Managing
anu
Sixth Form Colleges

Editor: Simon Lambert

Contributors
Frank Ansell, Principal, South Trafford College; John Baker, Principal, Brockenhurst College; Stephen Bennion, Dean, Yeovil College; Jackson Hall, former Director of Education, Sunderland; Simon Lambert, former Staff Inspector, HMI Education and Training 16–19; Peter Lineham, former Director of Studies, North Devon College; Shaun McLoughlin, Principal, Oswestry College; Rob Stephenson, Principal, Stoke on Trent Sixth Form College.

Longman Group UK Limited
Longman House, Burnt Mill, Harlow, Essex, CM20 2JE

British Library Cataloguing in Publication Data

Managing tertiary and sixth form colleges.
  1. Sixth form colleges—England—
  Administration   2. Universities and
  colleges—Great Britain—
  Administration
  I. Lambert, Simon
  373.2'38'068   LB2901

ISBN 0–582–02484–6

Printed and bound in Great Britain by
Biddles, Guildford, Surrey

CONTENTS

Acknowledgements   iv

Foreword   v

1   Introduction   1
    Simon Lambert

2   The management of change – a case study   13
    Jackson Hall

3   The process of change – the college viewpoint   27
    John Baker

4   Control and communication in the college   35
    Frank Ansell

5   Guidance and counselling in post-16 colleges   48
    Stephen Bennion

6   Liaison in post-16 education – an essential ingre-   58
    dient
    Peter Lineham

7   The curriculum and its delivery   77
    Rob Stephenson

8   Staff development   102
    Shaun McLoughlin

9   Postscript   118
    Simon Lambert

Acknowledgements

The editor and contributors wish to acknowledge, with thanks, the generous assistance of Paul Skates, Noel Kershaw, Ann King and David Holman.

Foreword

Colleges planned and established for the post-compulsory age group (16–19) have been in operation for some time; the first sixth form college in the maintained sector was opened in Luton in 1966 and the first tertiary college was opened in Exeter in 1970. Arguments on the political and educational background to these types of college continue, but the specific and particular problems of their establishment and management are seldom isolated from the emotions of their conception. This series of contributions attempts to remedy this deficiency and, at the same time, underlines the common purpose and the similarities between sixth form and tertiary colleges.

Simon Lambert
December 1987

1   Introduction

Simon Lambert

The development of the 16–19 colleges

The concept of an institution designed with the needs of the
16–19 year-old student in mind appears to have originated
in the late 1950s, although there are whispers of such
thoughts echoing back to before the last war. Since the
establishment of county grammar schools, as a result of the
1902 Education Act, it had been accepted by local education
authorities, schools, parents and students that there was a
logical progression through the educational system up to the
school leaving age, at which point the students left school
for employment or entered a sixth form. Those who took the
latter course were assumed to have ambitions towards
higher education and were selected for the sixth form on
their ability to achieve this aim. The relatively small number
who entered colleges of further education on full-time
courses were the exceptions and those who, while in
employment, enrolled on part-time courses in FE were seen
as trainees rather than students. The first of these assumptions to be challenged was the inviolable right of the schools
to be the sole providers of academic courses for the able
youngster, and only for them. For many years there had
been part-time courses in colleges of further education,
usually held in the evening session, for those wishing to
improve on their school leaving attainments; opportunities
to retake Ordinary level General Certificate of Education
(GCE O) subjects were on offer, and in many colleges it was
possible to continue further to Advanced (A) level GCE. The
departments in the colleges that offered these courses were
in the shadow of the larger, high status, vocational sections,

but they were, nevertheless, there and were providing an alternative to the schools. Thus the monopoly of the school sixth form was beginning to be eroded.

In 1954, members of Croydon Council set up a subcommittee to study the problems in the borough created by a growing population and the pressure for more grammar school places. Later, in the same year, the chief education officer produced a memorandum for this subcommittee in which he proposed that all the secondary schools in the borough should be able to offer GCE O level courses, and that the existing grammar school sixth forms should be combined to form a junior college where A level courses would be provided. This plan, as one would expect, was opposed by the heads of the grammar schools who produced all the arguments against the loss of their sixth forms which have become so familiar over the succeeding years: discontinuity of teaching between the fifth and sixth years; the desire of teachers to teach at all levels and the difficulties in their recruitment if this was denied them; and the concept, inherited from the public schools, that sixth formers should provide leadership and monitorial authority. The proposals were rejected by the education committee; the idea that the needs of students should be considered before the perceived needs of institutions was too radical for the time and the entrenched beliefs of the grammar schools were still too strong. Another attempt was made in Croydon in 1961; the same opponents emerged, the Ministry of Education (as it then was) showed little enthusiasm and the main architect and supporter of the scheme, the chief education officer, retired. Croydon did not, therefore, establish their junior college.

The first genuine sixth form college in the state sector opened in Luton in 1966, followed by the Southampton colleges in 1967. The number of colleges being opened increased rapidly, particularly between 1972 and 1980, and has now reached 105. Many of the early colleges were selective in their intake in that they concentrated on A level work; they could have been called 'grammar school sixth forms writ large'. This was understandable as they had to still the fears of parents who had been subjected to the protective propaganda of the grammar, and by now comprehensive, school heads in the period prior to re-organisation. However, as the new colleges became established and showed their worth, this situation soon changed. There had always been a group of students who had stayed on at school after 16 to improve their O level qualifications; traditionally, they had often been refused sixth form status and privileges and they were, indeed, a deprived minority. The social advantages of the emerging sixth form colleges were obvious and attractive to students of all abilities; many of this non-A level group began to apply to the new institutions and soon they were beginning to form a significant proportion of the colleges' population. Stimulated by the proposals from the Schools Council for a set of new courses and examinations for this group of students and by a legitimate desire to provide a fully comprehensive curriculum, most colleges became open access. The policy was successful; many students who, in the past, would have been rejected by school sixth forms flourished in the climate of the colleges and went on to take A levels or vocational courses in further education. This continuing progress was hindered only by the refusal of the Department of Education and Science to acknowledge and validate the courses developed by the Schools Council for these students – the Certificate of Extended Education (CEE).

At the same time, the demands for a more vocationally linked curriculum were becoming evident and the sixth form colleges, with average rolls of over 500, were in a position to respond. Schools had offered low level secretarial studies to their 4th and 5th year students for many years and the colleges were able to build on these foundations. They extended their courses, despite the opposition and objections of the further education service, within a number of pre-vocational areas. The same factor, i.e. their size, enabled them to support a series of non-traditional O level (AO) subjects and to be responsive to the introduction of the Advanced Supplementary (AS) level. From institutions that, in the 1960s, were not unlike large sixth forms, by the 1980s the sixth form colleges had established an identity and philosophy which was now firmly student centred.

The existence of the developing colleges had been acknowledged, although somewhat reluctantly, by the DES in circular 10/65 which suggested their formation as one of a series of schemes of secondary reorganisation. However successive Secretaries of State, from both right and left of the political spectrum, failed to grasp the real significance of the move toward 16–19 colleges. The left appeared wedded to the all-through (11/12–18) comprehensive school, while the right, or a major portion of it, could not cast off the nostalgia for the academic sixth form. The Inspectorate was equally enigmatic, showing no real support for the colleges and with a leadership in the secondary group who were clearly pro-sixth form.

During the debates on the establishment of sixth form colleges and during their development, many colleges of further education had been expanding their range of courses to satisfy what they saw as an increasing demand for school type work, i.e. GCE O and A level, in institutions which were being run on more informal lines than schools, without many of the disciplinary constraints that were essential when 11–16 pupils were present and where students could be given more control over their work and behaviour. Despite these developments, the FE colleges were still mainly vocational in their outlook and the large departments of engineering, construction, business studies and catering still had the most influence, but the fledgling general education departments were expanding and offering a wider range of courses to full-time 16–19 year-old students. Within these colleges there was still a tendency to overteach, the systems of student care and guidance were not as controlled or as effective as those that operated in the schools and the academic quality of many of the 16–19 students was only average; the schools fought hard to keep their able students. The scene was therefore ripe for competition for students, especially given the points system which made 16+ students so valuable to schools in terms of resources and staffing. Further education became the unmentionable topic at schools' careers evenings and, except for the very few who insisted on following the vocational road to higher education and training, potential students with any ability were guided, or led, to the school sixth form. Where sixth form colleges had been opened the competition was equally fierce. The only ameliorating feature here was that when schools no longer had sixth forms the staying-on rate into continuing education and training increased, often dramatically, and so there were many more potential students available for recruitment. Unfortunately, many schools pre-conditioned their pupils, advising them to attend the sixth form college if they were of the calibre that, in the past, would have given them entry to the sixth form. It was not unknown for staff from a sixth form college, visiting a school to describe their courses, to speak to the entire fifth year. A similar meeting, arranged for the staff from FE, would be attended only by those pupils that the school had decided would not be attending the sixth form college. The system was still institution biased, not student centred.

Onto this scene, in 1970, emerged a new type of institution – the tertiary college. The planning for this new concept began in Exeter after an abortive attempt to introduce a sixth form college, and in 1968 it was proposed that all post-16 work should be located in the newly rehoused Exeter Technical College. This plan was approved locally and then by the Secretary of State at the DES in August 1969. The idea of the tertiary college is an interesting one as, legally, they cannot be separated from any other FE college. They are simply colleges of further education which provide all the post-16 courses – full- and part-time, vocational and non-vocational – in a particular area. Voluntary schools often continue to keep their sixth forms, or establish aided sixth form colleges, and the independent sector is untouched.

The tertiary college is clearly derived from Lord Alexander's concept of a tertiary sector, where all post-16 education and training could be concentrated and which would be fully comprehensive. His proposals have, sadly, never been wholly implemented and only an outcome of them, the tertiary college, has survived and, indeed, flourished. The number of these colleges has increased steadily, though not as rapidly as the sixth form colleges, until, in 1987/88, there are 50 operating in England and Wales (Scotland has not yet entered the field). In their early days, all, with only one exception, were based on an existing FE college and an amalgamation took place with the local sixth forms. This gave the impression of an FE takeover – something that is far from the truth, although some staff in

FE have to be persuaded of this. Neither are they simply a fusion of further education and the sixth forms; they are new institutions with new ideas and practices. It has to be admitted that the reasoning of LEAs in their planning of tertiary colleges is rarely, if ever, totally educational. More often, they are persuaded by the long-term economy of a single, relatively large institution, the need to react to the decreasing size of the 16–19 age group and the effect of this on the ability of the sixth forms to remain viable and the changing nature of potential student's 16+ choice of courses. These factors help to explain the politically neutral attitude towards this form of reorganisation of those areas where the early colleges were established. Only when the tertiary concept became more popular did the political left see it as a reflection of their ideology; the right saw it as a threat to their elitism.

The undoubted success of the early tertiaries (14 of them up to 1979) began to influence the position of the sixth form colleges. Already, in the 1970s, in Preston and Richmond-on-Thames sixth form colleges had been closed and their students incorporated in new tertiary institutions. This process has continued and 11 of the more recent colleges include in their ancestry a sixth form college. This has, again, brought into focus the need for a clear distinction between the tertiary and the traditional FE college. The essential nature of these new colleges can be summarised as follows:

1. Because they are the major 16+ provider in a local area they are fully comprehensive, socially and academically, offering courses to all potential students over 16 and all abilities, so developing an affinity with all members of the local community.
2. They are able to offer potential students a choice of course which is unhindered by a parallel choice of institution; there are, therefore, no pressures on a student to remain in a school and help to maintain a diminishing sixth form or to transfer to a sixth form college.
3. Because they are FE colleges there are opportunities, rarely available when there is separate school provision,

for students to take a mixture of vocational and non-vocational subjects in their chosen courses.

4. As the majority of the students are under the age of 19, a large number of which are on full-time courses, the colleges design and operate sophisticated and effective tutor group systems giving their students support, guidance and care in ways that are as good, and often better, than those found in school sixth forms.

5. For many students the tertiary college is the sole provider of post-16 education and training, so the development of close links with local secondary schools is vital. A partnership evolves where the school pupils see the college as a normal part of their educational progression and where staff from both institutions work together with a common purpose.

6. The colleges are managed in such a way, either implicitly or explicitly, that a college ethos develops through college-based, rather than departmentally-based policies.

The political framework and the role of central government

By the late 1970s the sixth form monopoly had been broken; young people who wished to continue their education and training after their period of statutory school attendance could be found in the two kinds of institution described in the earlier part of this section, as well as in the schools and the traditional further education colleges. This variety did not, nor was it planned to, produce equality of opportunity. For some students the large sixth form, with its continuity from the main school, provided an adequate academic environment through A level courses, but for those with fewer or lower grade 16+ qualifications the opportunities were minimal.

The small sixth form was unsatisfactory for both groups; even fewer subjects were on offer for the A level student and the small size of both the total sixth and the individual teaching groups affected the examination results. This latter factor was confirmed by the DES in their statistical Bulletin

8/81. The sixth form colleges were producing A level results that were well above the national average for the maintained sector, and their CEE students were taking the opportunities offered by the new set of courses to remedy their relative lack of success at 16+. However, the competitive nature of the institutional choice at 16+ was still evident. Except in two or three areas, there were still not enough tertiary colleges to provide the comprehensive tertiary sector that Alexander had proposed.

A political dimension was now introduced as the emotions of those who supported the retention of school sixth forms began to be seen as a vote catcher, at least in local elections, and the comprehensive egalitarian picture of the tertiary college attracted the attention of others. Unfortunately, the sixth forms without recourse to setting up separate post 16 institutions, a number of schemes were, and still are, tried; added advantage of size; a number were established on these grounds. Some of the sixth form colleges were, undoubtedly, seen by their progenitors as an evolutionary step towards tertiary colleges and some of these have indeed since changed their status.

It very soon became clear that the central issue was not the colleges – sixth form or tertiary – that excited the interest, but the obvious fact that these colleges could not be established without restricting the age range of the secondary schools to 16. To try and overcome the problems of small sixth forms without recourse to setting up separate post 16 institutions, a number of schemes were, and still are, tried; sixth form centres, consortia, joint sixth forms and 16+ linked courses with FE. All of these tend to founder on two factors: firstly, some of the schools must give up some of their autonomy in sixth form matters and, secondly, it has become obvious that students dislike travelling to other institutions for part of their courses. The first of these factors is the most important and controversial as the possession, and possession is the right word in this context, of sixth formers is seen by many teachers as the crowning glory of the school. Anything that diminishes the sixth form is seen as adversely affecting the whole school, so any co-operation which might involve the loss of students to another school is avoided or circumvented. This explains why, apart from a small number of joint sixth forms where the local geography is convenient, the great majority of co-operative efforts fail to achieve any significant results.

The position of central government, as represented by the DES, had been quite clear during the development of the new-type colleges. Their responsibility was set out explicitly in the Education Act of 1944 which requires LEAs to secure the approval of the Secretary of State before any secondary school could be closed. Normally when a scheme of secondary reorganisation was to be implemented, whether it involved the formation of a 16–19 college or not, this approval had to be sought. This procedure, which was restated and extended in the Education Act of 1980, can be time-consuming and complex. Public notices have to be published in specified ways and places, objections to the scheme received and verified by the LEA, answers to these objections prepared and, finally, a submission made to the DES. As time has passed the amount of extra information that the civil servants in the DES have required an LEA to provide has increased, both in total amount and in detail. They, in turn, go through an equally time-consuming process to produce their advice for the Secretary of State and so the period of time that elapses between the formation of a scheme by an LEA, its submission to the DES and its ultimate acceptance, or rejection, by the DES can become alarmingly long. The factors that influence the Secretary of State's decision are obviously multifarious and the political views of the party in power form only part of the picture. Local feelings, as represented by the objections, lobbying by councillors, the views of the teacher unions and the effect of a proposed reorganisation on the government's policies on, say, the reduction in the number of pupil places, all have a place in the final consideration of an LEA's proposals. It is an interesting omission that statements of approval for a proposal, as opposed to objections, are not asked for and are rarely submitted spontaneously. It is also an anomaly of the legislation that, when it is suggested that a tertiary college is to be set up, the only apparent concern of the DES is the possible effect of the new system on the secondary schools. Clearly FE interests are considered, but there is no legal requirement to obtain them in any formal manner. This situation gives an undue advantage to the schools branch in the DES, as they co-ordinate the information on which the Secretary of State finally makes his decision.

Her Majesty's Inspectorate are also involved; HMI based in the locality where the proposals emanate are consulted and their opinion canvassed. In schemes which are planned to set up sixth form or tertiary colleges the views of the chief inspector for secondary education clearly carry weight. When holders of this post have little or no experience outside the 11–18 sector, and it is likely that their experience will have been restricted to this sector, then their view of 16–19 colleges may well be limited and this can have an effect on the final decision of the DES. Like the DES itself the Inspectorate is clearly divided into school and FE sections, but in 1978 the then senior chief inspector established a 16–19 group of three staff inspectors and a supporting team of HMI to oversee all 16–19 developments. The work of this group was divided, not on an institutional basis but according to the courses available, i.e. full-time, part-time or MSC-funded, and for some years this group produced a series of 16–19 reports. They also organised an annual conference on post-16 organisation and curriculum, which was based on the concept of a common philosophy for all 16–19 students—it attempted to break the vocational/non-vocational divide. In 1982, as one of a series of studies on the work of different branches of the civil service, a management review of the work of the Inspectorate was published. One of its recommendations was that a post of chief inspector should be established to take charge of the co-ordination of all aspects of work in relation to 16–19 education. This recommendation was never implemented and, on the retirement of the senior chief inspector in 1983, the old system was reinstituted, the forward-looking 16–19 group disbanded and the schools/FE divide reconstituted.

Before 1980, most plans for reorganisation which involved 16+ colleges were clearly part of schemes of secondary reorganisation along comprehensive lines and the stated views of the national political parties, in, for instance, any election manifesto, carried considerable weight. Nevertheless, educational factors were always given a priority, in particular the views and the experience of an LEA making the proposal. The outcome of this method of decision-making can be seen when the number of grammar schools being closed and the number of comprehensive schools being opened in their places, between 1970 and 1974, is studied. After the 1979 election, it became more evident to the DES ministers that the so-called 'jungle' of 16–19 provision and its use by students was becoming too complex and that the inter-institutional competition was working against the best interests of young people. A committee, chaired by a junior minister of the DES, Neil Macfarlane, was set up to report on these issues. Unfortunately, this report, when published, apparently failed to understand or accept the realities of the situation, either educationally or economically.

The report in its penultimate form, accepted by the members of the committee, set out to establish three principles:

1. That the needs of students come before the needs of institutions.
2. That the local authorities were in the best position to rationalise their own provision in their own way.
3. That small sixth forms were not only non-economic but were also unsatisfactory in educational terms.

However, when the report finally appeared there had been some major alterations to the text; a last ditch defence of the school sixth form was written in, spurious evidence on the difficulties of staffing 11–16 schools which fed into 16–18 colleges was inserted and systems with a mixed economy of 11–16 and 11–18 schools, despite the known failures of this method of organisation, were emphasised as a solution to the problem of small sixth forms. Thus, the report of the committee lost any sense of realism that it might have had, and what could have been a landmark in the planning of the education and training for the 16–19 student is now largely forgotten.

Since 1980, the minds of LEA committees and their officers have been sharpened and stimulated by a number of factors: in the early 1980s the number of 16–19 year-olds in the population began to fall and will continue to fall into the 1990s; youth unemployment and the measures taken to alleviate its effects have influenced the providing institutions;

pre-vocational education and training has become an
accepted and respectable major part of the 16–19 curriculum
and the success of the existing new colleges has, to some
extent, defused the opposition to them. The DES has
admitted that small sixth forms (with fewer than 150 pupils)
are unsatisfactory and it has become less overtly antagonistic
to sixth form and tertiary colleges, although the stated
intention of protecting sixth forms of 'proven worth' – a
characteristic not clearly defined – is still a factor that has to
be considered before reorganisation plans are submitted.
Similarly, the report published by the Centre for Policy
Studies, which opposed the break at 16, supported school
sixth forms and 11–16/11–18 mixed systems and cast doubts
on both sixth form and tertiary colleges, should not be
entirely forgotten as echoes of its conclusions are still heard
on occasion from some in the DES.

The areas of concern should now be focused on the tertiary
and sixth form colleges themselves. These colleges provide
courses for the education and training for 30 per cent of all
full-time 16–19 students in England and Wales. It is no
longer a question of 'if they are established' but how they
are established and how they are managed.

The possibility of some sixth form colleges over-concen-
trating on their more able students, the competition that still
exists between institutions, the difficulties of the 'sole
provider' concept of the tertiary college, the optimum as well
as the minimum and maximum size of the colleges and their
management and style are all factors needing continued
study.

2 The management of change – a case study

Jackson Hall

Introduction

A calendar of the course of events culminating in the approval by the Secretary of State of a scheme to establish a tertiary system in Sunderland is set out on pages 23–5. The scheme reduced the number of county secondary schools from 20 to 14 (with consequential changes in catchment areas affecting many primary schools), terminated sixth form provision in schools and doubled the sizes of the two colleges of further education. It might reasonably be assumed that change on this scale would be highly controversial and arouse bitter opposition. In fact, the scheme attracted general support and it was approved by the Council with only three members voting against it.

To secure general support for a radical change of policy with such far-reaching consequences can only be regarded as a success, and much of the credit for this success must be given to what is described here as a procedural policy. In a public, democratically-controlled service, a policy change requires attention to process, as well as concern about decisions; reorganisation schemes have foundered on some failure of process, regardless of the merits of the policy decision. Process, which is about how things are done, is associated with administration and policy is associated with management, which is where and how decisions are made. Each of these terms, administration and management, has a different resonance; administration sounds pedestrian and procedural, whereas management has a dynamic ring suggestive of decision and change. In the education service, however, the management of change should be a partnership of administration and management. It is this partnership which is the basis of the procedural policy. A procedural policy utilises process, and any explanation of the general support for the change must give much of the credit to the fact that the policy emerged from the process which led to its formulation. This is interesting because it suggests that, in some circumstances, it may be appropriate for the leadership element of management to be recessive. It was not the case, of course, that management was wholly recessive. Its representatives made it very clear from the beginning that changes would have to be made and that, at the very least, there would be some school closures and amalgamations. The firmness in this respect focused the discussion on the question of change; the item on the agenda was change and the issue was what the change should be.

The majority party was responsible for the status quo of 1979; the decision to change it did not stem from dissatisfaction with the status quo but was as a result of falling rolls. In short, falling rolls came as a deus ex machina, as a practical problem that had to be tackled but that could be resolved successfully in terms of educational advantage. In this situation, it was reasonable to consider the policy options on a pragmatic as distinct from an ideological basis. Furthermore, this approach reflected the instincts and nature of the majority party, whose basic ideological commitment was to the interests and well-being of the community, especially the less fortunate, rather than to abstract principles or theories of organisation.

The process

A laisser-faire policy for falling rolls is indefensible and it is the director of education's responsibility to advise. The choices seemed to be to seek a policy decision, to advise the education committee to appoint a working party or to explore a procedural route to a decision. This procedural route was not charted in detail initially, but three main phrases, each including public consultation, were envisaged:

1. Presentation (first to the committee and then publicly) of the facts and consequences of falling rolls and the policy options for dealing with the problem.
2. Presentation of what each of the policy options would mean in practice, so that discussion and consideration of their relative merits would be firmly anchored in reality.
3. Formulation of a scheme of reorganisation and its submission.

This procedure by phases, with public consultation at each stage, certainly complied with the relevant legislation. It was also strategically sound – each phase was a logical and progressive step to the next. Thirdly, the procedure left the policy decisions to the final phase by which time the information base for a judgement would be fully exposed. Fourthly, it offered at least the possibility of postponing any serious dissension – and limiting it – to the final phase, the most suitable time for it if it had to be faced. Finally, it respected the responsibilities of the members by leaving them free to launch a political initiative at any time.

In the event, the procedural policy was pursued and this was the route which led to the decision for a tertiary system. This strategy was not, however, fully articulated at the outset; although it was described in broad terms, no specific commitment was made and there was certainly no use of the term 'procedural policy' – the journey was travelled stage by stage, and political approval was sought at each stage.

A different level was tapped in ascertaining political approval for the second and third phases. For the first phase, which was expected to be controversial but unlikely to be divisive (since it was no more than a learning and familiarisation stage), the route taken was through the schools' governing body, which met in private, to the schools' sub-committee, which met in public. It could only be assumed, however, that the second and third phases would be divisive as well as controversial and in each case, the director consulted the chairman of the education committee and the leader of the council; on each occasion, the leader of the council convened a meeting of his senior colleagues (the chairman of the committees of the council), which was also attended by the chief executive, the treasurer and the director of administration, as well as the director of education. These meetings were decisive but not lengthy; their purpose was to test whether there was general support for the launch of the next phase and, apart from this, the discussion revolved around procedure, arrangements and timing. There was never any attempt to alter the papers provided by the director and, from his point of view, these meetings were most useful; despite some anxiety about them beforehand, the advantage of having the procedure considered and agreed in advance was considerable. As far as this dimension of the management of change was concerned, the respective functions of the leader, the chairman and the director of education – which, although distinct and different, must be complimentary – were effectively co-ordinated.

Timing

Although the procedure was started in good time, the time it took to complete it is open to criticism. Such delays are not unknown on policy issues. The fact is that work at this level falls on a few senior officers who are heavily committed to the day-to-day management of a demanding service which has suffered particular difficulties in recent years because of restrictions on public expenditure, contraction, new initiatives, new legislation and persistent disruption. This comment is not offered as an excuse but rather to underline a weakness, i.e. the vulnerability of the professional administrative cadre (the locus of professional planning in an education department) to other demands on its time and attention, demands which may well be less important but which are more urgent and must therefore be given priority. The difficulties of this cadre during these years were exacerbated by a high turnover.

What is not always appreciated about a calendar of this nature, however, is that its year is considerably less than 12 months. Meetings with the teachers' representatives and the public have to be held within the school terms. Secondly, the director of education's timetable for controversial issues was September to (at the latest) January, and the end of May to July to avoid the campaign season of the annual local elections. The chairman and the leader of the council may not have known this but the calendar illustrates its influence. These timetable factors are a constraint on the management of change.

The consultations

The exhaustive consultations at each stage were a salient feature of the strategy for change. There were 20 public meetings in phase 1, 42 in phase 2, and 20 in phase 3. It is not known how many other meetings were held, but every invitation to an officer to speak was accepted. The reports of the director which were the basis for the consultations were well-publicised and widely distributed. For phase 2, 60,000 area pamphlets, brief guides to the alternative policies and their possible applications in practice, were distributed. These popular guides (produced, in fact, at the suggestion of the leader of the council) were particularly helpful and appreciated. The frankness and thoroughness of the consultation were an essential arm of the procedural strategy and unquestionably contributed to its success.

The phasing of the consultations was undoubtedly sensible and helpful. At the end of phase 1, the fact of falling rolls and its consequences had been widely accepted; by the end of phase 2, there was general agreement that all the options had been identified and it was also clear that the 16–19 provision was a major issue; before the end of phase 3, the movement of opinion generally in favour of a tertiary system was pronounced. It would have been possible to telescope the whole process by producing a single, comprehensive report dealing with the problem of falling rolls, the policy options and their applications, and concluding with a recommendation; this would have been less exhausting, and theoretically a shorter process too, but the risks would have been very much greater, if only because there would have been a natural reaction against it. It would have given the impression that the decisions had already been made and, indeed, if management has virtually completed its thinking before it consults, the decision will almost certainly have been made. Parents and those in the service naturally feel very strongly that they have a right to contribute to and to influence change. Management has no justification for believing it knows best without first having listened to what people have to say, and very great care was taken to give full account of the opinions expressed at the public meetings in reports to the education committee. The scheme approved by the council in 1985 was influenced by views expressed in the public meetings – a feed-back is valuable to management.

Change and reassurance

Most of us value permanence and security; even the prospect of change is unsettling and unwelcome. Furthermore, to put change on the public agenda suggests that current arrangements are unsatisfactory. This worries parents, and teachers feel threatened by impending reorganisation and are aware that the need for change implies some inadequacy. In such circumstances, management has a particular obligation to maintain confidence and provide reassurance.

The fact that no significant change can be made without the approval of the Secretary of State may be reassuring to parents. This safeguard was, therefore, always emphasised at the public meetings, where it was explained that his decision would be made on the basis of his view of the best interests of the pupils, and in the light of advice given by civil servants at the DES and HM Inspectors whose independence and standing as professional educationalists were always underlined. This statutory provision for a second and informed judgement also emphasises the fiduciary nature of the educational responsibilities of both the LEA and the Secretary of State, and that the touchstone of decision is the community's best interests as distinct from some partisan criterion. Reassurance on this score was reinforced by an explanation at every meeting of the rights of objectors to the proposals.

What people at public meetings commonly feel is a sense of powerlessness; this breeds a healthy resentment, all the more deeply felt because it is their children's interests which are at stake. These statutory provisions assure them, at the very least, that the verdict does not rest with one court alone and that public interest is recognised and legally safeguarded. A difference in the political colour of the local and national party in power probably enhances the public valuation of the safeguard.

The 'us and them' gap, the distance between those who plan and those who will be affected by the planning, is always an obstacle and every effort was made to reduce it, even in small ways. For example, a large platform party is psychologically threatening in these circumstances, and for these meetings it never consisted of more than one member and one officer; at the end of every meeting, members and officers remained in the hall to meet those who, for one reason or another, preferred to speak in private. The frequency, frankness and the thoroughness of the consultations brought all those concerned more closely together.

The public documentation made it plain that the procedure was open and above-board, that the alternatives had been thought of and thought through. This suggested care as well as competence. The 1983 consultative document and the area pamphlets outlined each policy option and every conceivable application of each. The test applied by the senior officers in scrutinising the texts was whether every possibility had been presented, even to the extent of including a proposal they knew would not receive a moment's consideration in any quarter. It was not just that anything less would have been deficient, but that any omission might have reflected incompetence or roused suspicion that information was being provided selectively for some undisclosed purpose; in either case the cost would have been some loss of assurance and confidence.

The strategy of allowing a policy to emerge by an open process must have tended to obviate resentment and accusations that children's futures were being determined by 'politics', or political or educational ideology. The case for change was presented as the need to safeguard and improve educational standards and opportunities. And of course, the case made was not change for the sake of change. It was the impetus in the shape of falling rolls that made change necessary. The fact that it was the future deficiencies of the system, and that the authority was responding in good time (despite the slippage in the timetable), was probably somewhat reassuring – certainly more reassuring than it would have been had the authority been slower off the mark.

With the objective of relieving parental anxiety, it was explained that the scheme had been designed to minimise disturbance. For example, as far as possible, pupils would complete their courses (both 11–16 and sixth form) without a change of school; where amalgamations were proposed, it was explained that the staff of the new school would be drawn largely from the closing schools; where school transfer was unavoidable, the third year was to be transferred in time to ensure an uninterrupted two year's study to 16+. Because of the concern expressed over the disadvantages of the 'break' at 16+, an assurance was given that the careers guidance and the school and college tutorial services would be co-ordinated to safeguard continuity across the 16+ frontier. Another message which the public meetings registered was the public stereotype of the college of further education as a course-centred (and by implication, non-caring) establishment; although untrue, this stimulated further thought on the pastoral system to be provided in the tertiary colleges.

The Burnham 'protection' clauses and the locally negoti-ated teacher's relocation agreement were explained in the belief that it could only be reassuring to parents to know that there are orderly and agreed policies for teachers affected by reorganisation.

The staff associations

Until the decision was made, the range of possible changes was so wide that negotiation with the teachers' representa-tives would have been so complex as to be unmanageable. Apart from agreement on general principles therefore, detailed negotiations with the teachers' representatives had to be left until the scheme was approved. This may have been an advantage in that an area of potential controversy was postponed. The procedural strategy tended to give the members a quasi-judicial role in the nature of keeping a watching brief until the time for decision; the meetings with the staff representatives were therefore with officers. The well-established consultative committees, whose composition included members, were not used for discussions about reorganisation issues. The officers met the teachers' representatives, the secondary school heads and the principals of the two colleges of further education regularly. All of these meetings were, essentially, to exchange information; there were no debates on the relative merits of the policy options, because the main arguments were summarised in public documents and there was nothing material to add to them.

There were no objections from the staff associations to the procedure followed by the authority. The NUT notified its preference for an 11–18 school system and NATFHE submitted statements advocating a tertiary system, but none of the associations took part in the public discussions. It seems possible that the 1983 consultative document may have been influential on this front too; had it been less comprehensive in scope, less compendious in its detail, and less even-handed in its discussion, there might well have been a claim that the teachers' associations had a contribution to make.

The DES dimension

Since any scheme adopted by the council would require the approval of the Secretary of State, it was clearly sensible to keep the territorial officer at the DES and HM district and divisional inspectors fully informed. This work was done entirely by the director or the deputy director of education. These discussions in no way influenced the course of events in Sunderland, nor did the Sunderland officers believe for a moment that they would influence the DES decision; the advantage sought for Sunderland was that the submission would reach the Secretary of State's desk more quickly if the civil servants and HMIs concerned had been kept informed. Shortly after the formal submission from the authority, the director and the deputy director of education attended a meeting at Elizabeth House, the London office of the DES, to explain the scheme and the thinking behind it to a DES team; this was thought to be a useful meeting.

Questions were asked in Sunderland about the Secretary of State's likely response to a tertiary proposal involving the termination of a number of relatively strong sixth forms. The only answer to this was that some tertiary proposals had been approved and others rejected. No LEA could contemplate with equanimity the possibility of having its proposals turned down by the Secretary of State, but it should, nevertheless, exercise and formally record its own judgement of the best interests of the service for which it is responsible.

Conclusion

The opposition to the scheme finally submitted was slight and localised. Given the high feelings that reorganisation schemes usually generate, and have done in the past in Sunderland, the experience in this case is unusual and much of the credit for achieving such substantial agreement to a major change of policy must be attributed to the procedural policy and to the open public consultation.

There is a very real risk that an account as brief as this may be misleading. There is a danger, for example, that management may be seen as manipulative. It must, therefore, be said that the members (as far as is known) and certainly the officers set out without any commitment to a particular policy. Even as late as January 1985, the director of education's report to the education committee recorded his uncertainty about proposals for the western third of the authority. On the other hand, there may be critics who would censure management's recessive posture on the grounds that management should chart the future and lead the enterprise into it; these critics emphasise the importance of leadership in achieving change. The fact is, however, that success is a convincing criterion of leadership.

Finally, it must be remembered that, just as management cannot sensibly be held wholly responsible for most failures, neither can it take all the credit for a success. Even if all that management has done is known, there is the imponderable contribution of what it has not done, sometimes because it deliberately decided not to – the contribution to success of what management does not do partly explains why management is so difficult to assess. Beyond this, there is also the contribution of all those who were not part of the management in the ordinary sense of the term, but who nevertheless contributed because their participation in the process of making a change was thoughtful and responsible too. All the meetings on reorganisation held during these years were characterised by anxiety, but also, no less emphatically, by thoughtfulness and a sense of community responsibility.

Calendar of events

Phase 1: July 1979–June 1983

1979
July
Report on the estimated admissions and rolls (up to 1990) at each of the 20 county secondary schools considered by the Governing Body of Schools (see note). Further report requested on the policy options for tackling the problems.

1980
November The Governing Body forwarded to the Schools Sub-Committee a report identifying four policy options:

1. Modification of the existing system, involving a reduction (by amalgamation and closures) in the number of schools and, possibly, a reduction in the number of schools with sixth forms.
2. A system of 11–18 secondary schools.
3. A system of 11–16 secondary schools and sixth form colleges.
4. A system of 11–16 secondary schools and tertiary colleges.

The latter three options also involved a reduction in the number of schools.

1981

January   The November Report was approved by the Schools Sub-Committee and subsequently by the Education Committee for publication as a basis for public consultations.

June/July Meetings between officers of the Education Department with Heads and Principals, teaching staffs, and representatives of the teaching and non-teaching unions. Twenty public meetings.

October   Report summarising the responses to the consultations considered by the Governing Body.

Phase 2: July 1983–August 1984

1983

July   Meeting (convened by the Leader of the Council) of the chairmen of the major committees to discuss a report of the Director of Education on 'Falling Rolls and the Reorganisation of Secondary Schools'. Agreed that the report should be published early in September as a 'consultative document' prepared by the Director of Education as a basis for consultation and included on the agenda for the normal meeting of the Education Committee later that month.

September Publication of the report. Meetings of officers of the Education Committee with Heads and Principals, teaching staffs, representatives of the teaching and non-teaching unions, and with representatives of the Sunderland Branch of the Confederation of Parent-Teacher Associations.

October/
December   Forty public meetings

Phase 3: September 1984–September 1985

September Meeting (convened by the Leader of the Council) of the chairman of the major committees to discuss a report of the Director of Education which summarised the issues for decision and indicated the practicability of the policy options.

1985
January   The Education Committee considered:

      a) a report of the Director of Education on all
         the consultations which had taken place,
         including individual reports on each of the
         public meetings: and
      b) the report of the Director of Education
         advising on the issues and indicating the
         practicability of the policy options.

      The Education Committee decided that these
reports should be published, announced that it
would have a special meeting in May, at which
it would formulate proposals for reorganisation
as a basis for a further round of public consultations, and that meanwhile, it would welcome
representations on reorganisation from individuals and organisations with views on the shape
it should take.

May   Special meeting of the Education Committee.
The committee considered a report of the
Director of Education which set out detailed
proposals for reorganisation and approved it as
a basis for further consultations. Meetings of
officers of the education department with Heads
and Principals, and with representatives of the
teaching and non-teaching unions.

June/July   Twenty public meetings.

July   Twenty meetings of the Governing Body of
Schools. Special meeting of the Education
Committee when it was agreed to recommend
to the Council that the reorganisation proposals
contained in the May 1985 report should (with
minor amendments agreed in response to views
expressed at the public meetings) be recom-
mended to the Council for its approval.

September   Special Meeting of the Council at which the
Education Committee's recommendations were
agreed for submission to the Secretary of State.

A note on the governing body of county schools

Sunderland was one of those LEAs which had, under the 1944 Education Act, decided to appoint a single governing body for all county primary and secondary schools. Apart from a number of 'new' primary schools which had come within the provisions of the 1980 Education Act, the single governing body arrangement for proposals emerged. Nevertheless, the governing body met 20 times in July 1985 so that the heads of each county secondary school could express and discuss his/her views on his proposals, and also convey to the governors the views of the staff of the school.

3 The process of change – the college viewpoint

John Baker

During the early years of life of a tertiary college it is crucial that the management always keeps clearly in mind the reasoning that led to their college being redeveloped, whether that redevelopment came about by amalgamation with another institution or as a single college changing status. It is all too easy to become immersed in the short-term procedures and decision-making, particularly since the colleges now have a number of paymasters, some of whom, by use of their monetary power, seek to enforce a curriculum pattern that will meet their particular aims as paymasters.

The decision to provide a tertiary college will have been made by an authority after consideration of a range of economic and educational factors. These will certainly have included some of the following: small sixth forms; shortage of specialist teachers; uneconomic competition between neighbouring FE and sixth form colleges; a desire to provide 'vocational' opportunity for all at 16+; limitations on sixth form curriculum development because of Burnham regulations and examination board requirements; a wish to provide a fully comprehensive service; rationalisation of buildings; the need to encourage adult use of expensive facilities and falling rolls.

The balance of the priorities of these and other local factors will determine both the type and extent of initial capital investment provided by an authority and the broad outlines of the management team's initial five-year or so development plan.

Two recent examples illustrate this point. Firstly, that of a long established sixth form college serving a widespread local rural community. That college had itself developed from a grammar school base and had had to persuade the community that it would continue to operate with its traditional high academic standards, and that it would gain rather than lose by the change. That sixth form college had expanded its academic courses to serve a very wide range of abilities and, in co-operation with the nearest local technical college some 12 miles away, had been able to offer basic vocational courses. Under Burnham regulations, it was unable to expand further and large numbers of young people had to travel for their chosen vocational courses. Those students placed a considerable strain on the colleges to which they travelled.

The decision to go tertiary was taken mainly to allow the college to expand and more fully serve its locality, to lessen the travelling then taking place and also to widen the age range that could use the facilities.

The capital input was therefore made in the vocational areas with some enhancement of provision for the administrative team.

The second example concerns the amalgamation of a sixth form college and a nearby FE college, the timing of the amalgamation being determined by the fortuitous retirement of both principals. In this case both academic and vocational provision were available and the priority for capital investment was seen to be to provide an architecturally high profile student/administration/teaching block to be the pivotal point of the newly developed college, whilst a more standard building programme gradually allowed the move to a one-site campus. At the same time inter-college competition could be eliminated.

Capital programmes apart, a tertiary college requires a larger support staff, both administrative and technical. This is partly because a tertiary college is virtually free-standing in its administration and does not have the services normally supplied to, say, a sixth form college from a local authority area office, and partly because the large increase in numbers bring with it considerable administrative needs. In addition, the much greater freedom to operate a more complex budget cost effectively brings with it the need to obtain the advice and help of financial officers. The advent of work-related non-advanced further education with MSC oversight, plus the need to make numerous bids to obtain special grants, have also added to the tertiary administrative load. Clearly, the widespread practical courses on offer bring with them the need for technical support staff.

The heavy increase of support staff required on changeover is made to seem yet more excessive by the very limited support staff in many sixth form colleges.

Undoubtedly the strain of change falls most heavily on the teaching staff, and there is really no chance of any smooth reorganisation taking place without teaching staff support. That support is more likely to be offered if all staff to be involved are kept closely in touch with the discussions and arguments prior to the change, and are thus able to see clearly the effects upon them as individuals.

The management approach to this challenge is certainly complicated by the traditional misunderstandings, between secondary and FE staff, of their respective roles. When an amalgamation is suggested each group believes that the other will be favoured: on one hand, that secondary academics will clearly be offered the plum appointments, whilst on the other, that experienced exponents of vocational courses will be given priority. The recent changes in schools' conditions of service will certainly have lessened the differences between the two sectors, but in any case the differences are more apparent than real. Because of the extraordinary division between the 'schools' and 'further education' sectors at all levels of our education service, a whole series of myths and beliefs have grown up. These are most acutely observed at teacher/lecturer level, mainly by the teachers or lecturers themselves. For instance, there is a widespread belief that the staffing structure of a further education college must be of vertical rather than matrix pattern. Again, concern is often expressed that within a further education college there is no freedom or opportunity for staff to exhibit their traditional school based skills and experience in the field of student care and guidance. Neither of these beliefs can be substantiated. The scheme of conditions of service, commonly known as the Silver Book, whilst clearly outlining the limits of the working year, teaching loads and class contact hours, in no way imposes these perceived limitations, although custom and practice in some long established colleges may encourage such speculation.

Nor, incidentally, do lecturers work far less hours for much greater pay. A comparison of the work load of a junior lecturer and the average secondary teacher destroys this misunderstanding. There is sufficient flexibility in any further education regulations or traditions for a tertiary college to operate elements of both styles of post-16 education and, indeed, this fact must be one of the great strengths of tertiary colleges.

All staff, when changes are afoot, will quite understandably wish to ensure that the quality of their working life is not lessened and will thus need to know their position, role, salary, promotion prospects and, that almost indefinable quality, status in the newly formed college.

It is a fairly simple matter to prepare and publish the proposed new staffing structure well before changes take place which, together with outline job descriptions, will allow individuals to determine position, role and, to some extent, promotion prospects.

Status within an organisation is more perceived than real, being mainly determined by the attitudes and actions of senior colleagues and is certainly not acquired, as a right, with a job title. An indication of likely status in a new institution can only be assessed by discussion with those who will be senior colleagues and, in any case, cannot be guaranteed.

Salaries, however, can be accurately predicted. Unless, most unusually, a decision is made to close institutions and open as new, then all salaries are protected so that no-one need worry about losing financially. The advent of the new schools salary structure and the likelihood of a restructuring of FE scales make it inappropriate to provide detailed examples, but an analysis of current and pending legislation shows that it is unlikely that the ground rules that now operate on changeover from schools to FE scales will be altered.

The salary on changeover from schools to further education depends, not on actual salary, but upon the relationship between the maxima of the previously held and new scales.

If an individual moves on to an FE scale whose maximum is greater than the schools scale previously held, then there is deemed to be a promotion. The new salary is obtained by adding $1\frac{1}{2}$ incremental points to the current salary and then slotting in to the point of the FE scale at or above that figure.

If the schools maximum is below that of the FE scale, then the salary is protected. For the purposes of such assessment the schools scale shall be deemed to be the 'main' scale plus any allowances held at the time of change to further education.

The staffing structure, upon which the success of the newly emerging tertiary college depends, needs to reflect its objectives and need not repeat the pattern established over the years by the 'traditional' technical college. These long standing colleges have evolved from their original need to provide a series of self-contained courses, each of which reflected the particular needs of an industry or commercial undertaking. The management structure reflected these responsibilities by providing a series of departments, each servicing clearly defined specialisms.

The tertiary college has to provide for the total local community and this need, together with the advent of many cross-curricular courses, requires a structure that gives applicants access to all opportunities available in the college. Strong, free-standing departments with their own admission procedures become irrelevant and, at worst, obstructive and expensive. A centralised admission and guidance procedure must have priority over in-house departmental autonomy.

To be successful, the tertiary college must set out to demonstrate to all sectors of the community that it provides every opportunity that was perceived to be on offer in the separate establishments. It has to show that it can achieve the academic success of schools and sixth form colleges, whilst assuring that it's vocational courses are as effectively staffed and equipped as those to be found in the larger technical colleges. It must show that it operates the quality of care and guidance associated with full-time institutions, whilst allowing the perceived 'non-school' style freedom sought by part-time, and many full-time, students. In addition, it must provide a warm and welcoming image to adults in the community who can thus be persuaded to resume their education and training.

In short, it must offer the best of all worlds, hence the need for a carefully orchestrated total college marketing role, which cannot be successful if there are signs of fragmentation and internal conflict. All staff must understand the role of the new college and be encouraged to play their part in welcoming students of all backgrounds to the college community.

Given some degree of success at this interesting task, the tertiary colleges can begin to solve some of the logistic and financial difficulties facing local authorities. Those tertiary colleges now in operation have, in their comparatively short life, all shared the one common characteristic of every sixth form college which opened during the last decade or so, that is an immediate growth in the percentage take-up from the school-leaving population. The growth in the tertiary colleges is well above that which can be related to the additional courses on offer.

This growth appears to be mainly brought about by what can be termed 'friendship factor', and this belief is confirmed by many of the heads of partner schools who feed into tertiary colleges. Although the function of a tertiary may require students to travel greater distances than previously, prospective students know that the majority of their friends will share the travelling time and also the college community. Careers advisers in the schools have found their task simplified because they may spend their time talking about the most suitable course without having to explain the differing venues that any particular choice would entail.

The greater flexibility in opening hours and the extended curriculum in 'their' local college seems to encourage adults in the community to be more confident about returning to study.

This growth in take-up is a particularly important factor at a time of falling rolls in schools and may be accentuated even more with the advent of a national TVEI curriculum, for clearly, the tertiary college is ideally placed to provide the progression paths required at 16 + by this initiative.

In any event, the links between schools and colleges, encouraged if not enforced by TVEI, can only be advantageous by allowing pupils to experience life in a 16 + college, where conditions are not adapted to the needs and control of 11–16 pupils.

Whilst this section has concentrated on the planning required to ensure that a tertiary college begins its life with a co-operative and well-informed staff, there must, from the very outset, be a great deal of forward planning. Very often, the first germ of the idea that finally leads to the provision of a tertiary college in an area comes about because of falling school rolls. Generally, the first response to such an imminent drop in numbers is to consider rationalisation of subjects and courses across the institutions in an area. Usually, after a great deal of analysis and time, the actual rationalisation is limited to a few minority A level subjects, and this almost totally within the school sector. It is difficult to rationalise such cost ineffective subjects in further education because of the need to keep opportunities open for adults. The tertiary college, however, with its large school intake and adult infill, is more likely to be able to keep minority subjects running and is certainly able to provide a high average class size figure across its community.

Even so, hard decisions have to be taken in tertiary as in all 16 + institutions. The range of single subject examinations on offer must keep open full career opportunities without wasteful duplication of similar subject titles. The selection of courses is becoming progressively easier as the emphasis moves towards somewhat less vocational specific titles.

For both single subjects and courses the tertiary college, carrying as it must a wide range to meet the total needs of the community, is ideally structured to take maximum advantage of the career gains and cost effectiveness of the modular elements now happily being developed.

The advent of MSC and its insistence on detailed forward planning has certainly brought a greater complexity to the life of college managers, but, in addition, has given further impetus to the drive that all tertiary colleges make to identify the needs of the community they serve. Without such knowledge, clearly, there can be no possibility of reasonably accurate predictions of trends and clientele so necessary for cost effective operations. This thought highlights the need to refer back to the concern expressed in the opening paragraph of this chapter. It would be so very easy for the management teams of a tertiary college to become so immersed in the technicalities of forward planning, management budgeting, unit costs, efficiency indicators and cost effectiveness that they leave insufficient time for consideration and guidance related to the college's real purpose. All students, particularly the large numbers of full-time students in the colleges, have a right to receive a fully rounded education that must include elements of staff time and commitment that cannot and should not be measured in any but educational terms. The tertiary colleges have shown that they have the opportunity and capacity to provide educational advancement and stimulation for all abilities and ages and at the same time keep within any reasonable financial limits. That the colleges demonstrate these factors from their opening illustrates the importance of forward planning which involves the staff – teaching, administrative and service – from the very beginning of the development of the new college.

4 Control and communication in the college

Frank Ansell

The present system of education for the post-16 age group is derived from two sources, the mechanics institutes and technical colleges on the one hand and the schools on the other. To understand the differing organisational forms it is necessary to consider their origins and purposes.

The first technical college to be established in England was at Finsbury in 1883. It was organised in five sections, by its acting principal Philip Magnus, to teach mechanical engineering, electrical engineering, technical chemistry, applied art and trade classes. The department was born.

For many years the department was the central unit of any college. The student came to the college to learn a single subject or discipline, say mechanical engineering. He would find himself in a department of mechanical engineering. Mechanical engineers would teach him all they needed to know to follow their chosen profession. Departments did not mix.

One problem area was the teaching of mathematics. The different forms of engineering all required mathematics, as did science. The building crafts required a variety of mathematics peculiar to its own needs. What would be more natural than that the subject specialists should teach the mathematics too? If specialist mathematicians were employed, surely they too would be located within the departments, working closely with the colleagues they needed to know and whose requirements they needed to understand. Alternatively, departments of mathematics could be created as a base for a team of mathematicians who would be leased out to the remaining departments. Since each such lecturer, servicing one other department, inevitably became more and more involved in this department there was little effective difference between the two systems and the mathematicians generally did not work as a team.

Another problem area arose after life returned to normal following the second world war, as technical education expanded rapidly and threatened to smother the arts, creating scientists and technologists with very narrow backgrounds. By the early fifties some colleges had begun to offer 'liberal studies' in an attempt to combat this tendency. The move attracted interest and support such that, in 1957, the Ministry of Education issued Circular 323 entitled 'Liberal Education in Technical Colleges'. The colleges tackled the challenge now presented in one of two main ways. Either they employed liberal studies staff in each department or, more commonly, they developed departments of liberal studies. The problems which arose were not the same as those which had occurred with the teaching of mathematics, but the newly established departments commonly set themselves up as discrete entities and did not usually see their purpose as liberalising the technical education taking place in other departments.

As time has passed, it has become the exception rather than the rule for students to study a single discipline. Many courses are termed multi-disciplinary or integrated. Business studies, for example, is an amalgam of communication studies, social sciences and number-based subjects, and those aspiring to careers in nursing study both natural and social sciences. How can these students be effectively taught in the departmental system? Traditionally, the answer has been to allocate the students to one department as a base while 'servicing' the course using staff from other departments. Thus, traditionally, colleges are course-based institutions.

In simple terms, schools have existed to provide a general education. Consequently, courses based on specific subjects have been very much the exception rather than the rule. All school courses are, in a sense, integrated. We talk of GCE courses meaning all the subjects being studied and we prefer to see such courses having a balance of different kinds of subjects. When a school talks of its departments it means those groups of staff who teach the same or related subjects to pupils (students) across the whole school

Generally, sixth form colleges have adopted the subject department structure found in schools for obvious reasons. Some have sought to reduce the problem created by the existence of many tiny departments through the introduction of a faculty structure. This is unlikely to present difficulties in the sciences or social sciences, but faculties of humanities contain many diverse interests and stresses can develop.

In recent years, schools and, more particularly, sixth form colleges, have been introducing discrete courses. Secretarial skills courses and business studies courses are the most common, and in these areas staff organisation can approach the FE structure in practice if not in theory.

Traditionally, however, schools and, therefore sixth form colleges, are student-based institutions. The development of the tertiary colleges has highlighted the fundamental differences between the two approaches traditionally adopted by schools and colleges. Neither completely satisfies the needs of these new colleges or, indeed, of those FE colleges which make a large general education provision. The purpose of these colleges is to provide the full range of educational experiences for the 16–19 age group and to make a major contribution to the provision of non-advanced further education for all those beyond 19 years of age. They must, therefore, provide both subject-specific courses and general education courses. The need to provide part-time courses by day and by evening for vocational and non-vocational study only serves to complicate matters.

How can this provision be made efficiently and effectively? Since tertiary colleges are, by regulation, classified as FE establishments there was initially, at least, a tendency to adopt a modified FE structure. It has already been suggested that this presents a number of difficulties. It is clear that the departmental system has been described as one in which the principal allows the head of department to run his department without interference. This would give him an opportunity to develop his department at the expense of students and other departments. It is not suggested that this is done maliciously or with utter disregard for the students, but the system does encourage such actions.

If staff are enthusiastic about their subjects they naturally wish to share that enthusiasm and encourage students to enrol with them. If they are successful the department grows bigger and many benefits accrue; more staff will be appointed, more senior posts will be established and the head will receive more support from these senior appointments and more salary as a result of the 'Burnham' arrangements. Everything supports the unthinking desire for growth and the quest for power. For power brings a larger share of the financial resources, a larger allocation of accommodation, more support for new and prestigious courses and, inevitably, yet more students. Weaker departments will suffer. Some students will benefit from this approach. The majority will not.

The reasons are not immediately obvious. Students will be attracted to courses by the power exercised by the department. More experienced and more senior staff will be more effective in recruiting for their courses. Better facilities, staff, accommodation and resources will provide better examination results and success leads to greater success and success attracts. The student is less likely to think about his real needs. The student who is well placed in a strong department will be in a good position. If badly placed or in a weak department the student will suffer.

The school structure does not serve us any better, for departments are many and small. It is inevitable that designated departments will tend to become separated from each other. Co-ordination of many small units is not easy. A solution commonly adopted is the introduction of faculties (aggregations of small departments of related disciplines), which may well produce the problems of the traditional FE structure if care is not taken. It is clear that a middle road is required. The author advocates a solution which uses the FE head of department posts to introduce a team of senior managers (or directors) to provide cross-college management while collecting the teaching staff into groups similar to school departments or small faculties. In this structure, each group (or section) is led by a senior lecturer and consists of staff teaching related (or at least not totally dissimilar) subjects across the college on any courses offered by the college. It is an important feature of this system that the senior lectures are seen to have similar work loads. In the same way, the directors have equal responsibilities. By this means, teamwork is encouraged and unhealthy competition is largely eliminated.

This structure is commonly called a matrix structure, though the term is not universally accepted as appropriate. Stated simply, it is very similar to a school structure but has, by virtue of its size and complexity, the added services of a team of specialist functional managers.

To find out how the departmental and the matrix systems compare it is necessary to examine the major activities of the managers in the system, whether they be heads of traditional departments or managers in a matrix.

Taking care of students

Students are attracted to the college by the image it projects. Communication with schools and the community at large must be of a high quality. This is most effective when centralised. A pupil joins a school, never a specific course within a school. It is quite usual, however, to talk of students joining college departments or college courses. It is frequently the case that student applications are directed to an individual department or even to a specific course tutor. Under this system it is not surprising that, if acceptable, students are enrolled in the department or on the course without always full consideration being given to their best interests. There may be other courses of which the student is not aware. There may be careers which the student has not considered. There will almost certainly be special options or variations of which the student is unaware. Even worse it may be that the head of department feels a need to enlarge his department and encourages his staff to maximise enrolments. The only way to solve these problems is to ensure that the student admissions are processed centrally and that interviewers assist the student to consider the full range of options. Even though tertiary colleges are, by definition, comprehensive institutions they will only be able to satisfy the needs of the majority of potential students. All colleges must, therefore, be prepared to advise students, when necessary, that it is in their own interests to consider courses in institutions other than their own.

Levels of pastoral care are notoriously varied in different colleges, but there are variations within a college. Obviously, this is necessary within a departmental system. If one manager is responsible for the whole of the care system common standards are more likely to be achieved, even though the system is operated by numerous individuals. An even more obvious problem is the probability that differing disciplinary standards will be adopted within a college. Again, standardisation is essential in a well run college.

Staffing matters

A major part of any head of department's work concerns staffing. Commonly, responsibility lies in preparing job specifications, advertisements, short-listing, assisting at interviews for appointment, inducting new members of staff, deployment, development (with or without formal appraisal) and discipline. Administration of staff timetables and part-time staff contracts are additional burdens.

In the departmental system the use by one department of the services of a lecturer from another department involves the agreement of two heads; the two departments have to harmonise at this point of contact. Such problems are removed by centralising these functions and by centralising timetabling.

Use and resources

Resources are limited throughout the educational service and must be conserved. The departmental system encourages equipment to be duplicated unnecessarily; it is not unknown for equipment to be lying idle in physics labs and in engineering science labs because two sets have been bought when only one was needed. Money is commonly allocated to departments on a historical basis and departments will spend beyond their requirements simply because the money is available, even if other departments are short. Not only should money be allocated according to present and future needs, rather than past needs, but its spending should be constantly monitored. Departmental timetabling leads to large classes being found in small rooms, while small classes are in large rooms.

All these inefficiencies can be avoided through better communication. It can be argued that people can still talk across departmental boundaries, but in a vertically divided organisation communication tends to run vertically. When a head of department is responsible for the happenings in his own department he is unlikely to encourage his staff to negotiate with staff of other departments without his knowledge. Only by removing or, at least, weakening the barriers can information flow, facilitating co-operation in the use of equipment, in timetabling and the efficient use of accommodation.

Curriculum

Central development of college provision is essential in these days of integrated courses, especially now that CPVE is with us, if the final programme offered is to be coherent, without duplication or unintentional omissions. Traditionally, it has been the responsibility of the academic board to consider departmental proposals and determine a final programme. One person, as in the matrix organisation, will be more effective than any committee in producing such a programme. This can then be approved by the board with relative ease.

Course and curriculum development is a specialised area of work. A single co-ordinator can streamline the work and produce schemes with a recognisable (and presumably satisfactory) house style. A comprehensive record of out-line schemes of work should be maintained centrally. A uniform style of presentation assists in the preparation, storage, retrieval and use of such schemes.

Marketing

Properly, marketing includes attention to the nature of the product, i.e. the course or curriculum and its quality. Here, the expression is used in the narrower sense of promotion. The production of promotional literature is yet another specialised activity. If centralised a true house style can be developed. Liaison requires a high degree of co-ordination if visits, in and out, are to be both effective and economical in terms of time and effort. Liaison with industry, schools and the general public are all part of the task, and again, a coherent package is essential. Effective promotion also entails the issuing of press releases, mounting exhibitions and other events and paying attention to such mundane matters as the general appearance of the premises and grounds.

Quality

A head of department spends considerable effort on ensuring the maintenance of standards. It is a task undertaken almost single-handedly. It is extremely difficult in the departmental system to ensure that standards are uniform across the college. The difficulty in the matrix structure is that the responsibility for quality control is less easily assigned to specific individuals. The easy answer is to say that all are responsible in their own way but, for this to be effective it requires a degree of conscientiousness which is not normally found and which is difficult to ensure.

These considerations lead us to the conclusion that the departmental system gives rise to a lack of co-ordination, as a result of difficulties in communicating across departmental boundaries and from the lack of necessity for such communication. If the head of department is allowed to run a department without interference, as has been suggested already, then it would not be advantageous to have free communication between departments. There may, therefore, be no will to change the system. Put less harshly, it has to be said that the early system, in which communication between departments was unnecessary, developed into one in which the heads of departments (the pirate kings of the service) saw a positive advantage in limiting opportunities to communicate. Now that resources are at a premium and integration is the 'name of the game' free communication is essential, despite being inhibited by the traditional structure. We can readily observe that throughout the traditional college responsibility, like communication, flows vertically, each member of staff being responsible to an immediate superior of a higher grade. Each person is responsible for the activities of their subordinates. There is intrinsic caution in the system. Action is not encouraged in this environment. The concept of hierarchy has to be broken down to ensure that full advantage is taken of the abilities of all staff. Older, more established staff have experience; they have seen the problems before. Newer staff have new ideas which they must be permitted to put into practice or to experiment with. Everyone must be made responsible for his own actions, while not being discouraged from developing new methods and new ideas.

The solutions devised for these multifarious problems appear to differ widely. In fact, they almost invariably have a number of common features:

1. The removal of rigid lines of demarcation, resulting in easier cross-college communication.
2. The centralisation of all activities not specifically related to small groups of courses, subjects, staff or students.
3. The creation of posts with college-wide responsibilities to operate these centralised activities.

The most successful institutions also make it abundantly clear that all staff, including the newest teachers and the ancilliary staff, have a significant role to play in the general well-being and running of the institution. No one can be excused from responsibility and everyone must be given the authority to act in line with their responsibility.

This then is the general framework. Certain advantages will be immediately apparent and these generally occur because systems and resources can be centralised. Rooms are no longer left idle because they belong to one department while another teaches theory in a practical environment. Departments will no longer purchase the same set of instruments unless they are used for more than six or eight hours a week. Staff are no longer frustrated by not being able to become involved in developments in another part of the college. Students are no longer debarred from studying in two departments and hybrid courses, such as CPVE, are no longer impossibly difficult to organise. The centralisation of certain activities is essential to the smooth running of the system. If a course programme is to be prepared within a college programme it must be prepared centrally. Individual course details are first prepared. Decisions, based on past experience and local market intelligence, are then taken regarding the programme to be offered. Only then can the timetable be produced. This work is co-ordinated by a senior member of staff using the knowledge and experience of specialist staff throughout the college. Courses and accommodation are put together first and staff allocated to the courses and classes last of all.

Two major benefits are derived from this system. No-one walks the corridors looking for alternative accommodation, only to find a week or two later that their newly acquired room had been allocated to another course whose start date had been delayed. The good and bad times of the day and the week and the good and bad accommodation are distributed far more fairly than any departmental timetabling can achieve. Student admissions are also centralised. Students on day-release need courses related to their work, but more and more students are enrolling for full-time courses. All applications are received centrally and all applicants are interviewed by staff chosen for their known ability or assumed ability as sound interviewers. Many students really do know exactly what they want. Such interviews are easy, but the interviewers need to ensure that all reasonable possibilities have been considered. In this way students are counselled and early information on likely demands on the system is obtained. Once this shows a real likelihood of a changing pattern of demand, changes can be made to the draft timetable. School leaving examination results come out in August. Only when these are known and assimilated can the final stage of the admission procedure begin. Some students do better than expected and some worse, some new applications are received and some early applicants lose interest, though not all students communicate this to the college. All new students should be reinterviewed in September. For many this is a formality, but for the majority unexpected examination results or a change of heart makes a fresh look at the proposed course of study desirable.

This procedure increases both efficiency and effectiveness. A constant watch can be kept on class sizes and the students can be confident that every effort has been made to enrol them onto the course that most suits their requirements. The vested interests of the interviewer in increasing the size of his classes are minimised. Even the bias resulting from a proper enthusiasm of an interviewer for his own subject can be reduced, though it cannot be removed and it would probably be wrong to attempt to go this far.

Centralised systems do not necessarily lead to centralised control. Many colleges abound with committees. Most colleges have an academic board established by virtue of their articles of government. Generally, this is the only committee that a college is required to have. Even so, committees flourish. While not denying the need for staff to meet to discuss many curricular and organisational matters, the author suggests that such meetings could be informal without the need for formal notices, agenda and minutes. When an extensive programme of formal meetings does exist, there is a danger that meetings are held simply because it is two o'clock on Wednesday rather than because there is something important to discuss. It is, perhaps, surprising that staff who will talk freely in an informal situation seem to be inhibited by the prospect of having the points they make minuted, but this seems to be quite common. A much more effective way of encouraging discussion and ensuring that staff do share experiences is to make time available for discussion, rather than have meetings. Some colleges arrange their timetables in such a way that a specific hour in the week is set aside for staff discussion. If this is arranged on a college basis rather than a departmental or sectional basis then, with a little ingenuity, either formal or informal subject and course meetings can take place. In this way staff can be enabled and encouraged to participate fully in decision making. Even if, as suggested, formal minutes are not taken it is still necessary to keep some formal record of decisions made. Even senior staff meetings can be informalised. In the federal or departmental system, there is a need to bring together the heads of department to ensure that a uniform approach is made to such matters as discipline and to discuss resource allocation. Since only the principal and vice-principal will have knowledge of the whole college they, either one or both, must be present at all meetings. When senior staff have functional roles each will be an expert in one aspect of college management; they can hold meetings with subject and course leaders without the presence of principal or vice-principal.

Senior staff meetings, then, have a different purpose from that in traditionally organised colleges. They can be more informal, as their main purpose is to ensure that the senior staff do not become isolated and that they know what the others are doing. They receive general information from one another, which is for general use, rather than making agreements or receiving instructions to which they have to conform. This system works well when everyone knows what their job is and is allowed to get on with it. Communications are essentially oral – written confirmation is only given when felt to be necessary. Some will argue that oral communication is unreliable. It could also be argued that a person who cannot remember what has been said is just as likely to forget what he or she has read, and to lose the piece of paper as well!

If, as has been suggested, meetings are informal and oral communication is encouraged, it might appear that staff will need to talk extensively to all and sundry while getting little else done. Such a view would be inaccurate; the talking would be extensive but it would be purposeful, being initiated by the talkers themselves who, with teaching commitments, have quite enough to do without wasting time. A few staff do have difficulty in using the informal communication network. They are not certain to whom they should talk in particular circumstances. This may arise when responsibilities are being exchanged or rotated around a group of staff, but it is generally due to an unwillingness to communicate freely. It really does not matter if the initial contact is with the wrong person. He or she will soon indicate the person who should be contacted. A thought worth sharing is worth sharing with anyone, since it is unlikely that the person approached will have no interest in the topic in question.

However, it must be admitted that while formality can stifle many, informality can frighten a few.

The picture emerging should be one of an academic community reducing bureaucracy and administration to a minimum, consistent with the provision of an efficient and effective educational service to students. Above all the needs of the students are paramount.

5 Guidance and counselling in post-16 colleges

Stephen Bennion

In the time it takes an eleven year-old to reach the final year of an 11–18 school, the post-16 college will have renewed its student population three times over. Brief associations, however, need not be superficial. Sixth form and tertiary colleges take pride in maintaining and building on the tradition of good pastoral care found in schools. Their internal organisation and management in many cases reinforce a commonly made claim to be student-centred institutions. An outsider, however, may puzzle over the existence of any system of pastoral care operating in a community made up of young adults who value their independence. Surely they are old enough to cope on their own? And so they do, often extremely well, for much of the time. On the other hand there are variations in maturity and the amount of support students may need. Post-16 colleges take the view that all young people value a helping hand, at one time or another, in sorting out problems or in coming to important decisions. Time spent in this way ranks highly amongst a college's priorities.

However willing they are, it is simply not possible for one or two nominated staff – vice principles or counsellors – to maintain regular contact with all students in a large post-16 college. Delegation must be the answer. A familiar way of directing attention to the needs of each young person is through tutorial systems. Like schools, many colleges identify the tutor as the lynchpin in their system of pastoral care. A member of the teaching staff, wearing a tutorial hat, carries responsibility for a group of students as they make their way through college. The relationship between tutor and tutor group should be a close one. A tutor gets to know his or her students better than anyone else, sees them in the round, as it were, not simply as BTEC engineers or A level historians, and is thus well placed to advise from a wide perspective. For their part, students come to look upon the tutor as the first point of contact whether the matter is administrative or personal, academic or vocational.

Typically, a group of tutors is responsible to a senior member of staff designated senior tutor, director or dean of studies or vice principal, whose time is divided between the admission of new students (sometimes from particular contributory schools), oversight of the tutorial programme and contact with individual tutors.

In a situation where one member of staff is answerable to another, questions arise over the boundaries of respective roles. Given a chain of command, a danger exists of tutors being reduced to the rank of ciphers; job satisfaction is diminished and professional expertise underused as decisions coalesce around one person. If, on the other hand, tutors are equipped to assume a clearly defined role and authorised to take the majority of decisions, students will find a great deal more accomplished on their behalf. Delegation of authority does not presage a retreat of senior staff. On very important matters consultation will take place before decisions are taken, however, senior staff may overrule a tutor on those few occasions when views diverge. In the main, a tutor's commitment increases when the scope of the job is known, when autonomy is granted and when worthwhile responsibilities demand attention.

Yet staff have only so much time for tutoring. Some hesitate to involve themselves in matters they believe lie outside their competence. With nowhere to turn for support paralysis would set in. Happily, the scale of most post-16 colleges enables specialist staff to be appointed whose main function is to complement the generalist. The small team, which usually goes by the name of student services, is made up of one or two careers advisers, counsellors (perhaps with responsibility for accommodation or finance) and often a chaplain, whether full- or part-time. Students contact student services on their own initiative or on the advice of their tutor. A professional counselling service, valued for its confidentiality, provides a second door for students to use in times of personal difficulty. As more calls are made on their time and as changing demands make themselves felt, student services are obliged to adapt. Specialist staff may take on a wider brief so that roles become, to some extent, interchangeable. Reappraisal will have succeeded if it enables the service to respond to more students (including a growing number of part-time adult students), many of whom, following initial advice or counselling, will be equipped to make their way independently.

However versatile the staff or extensive its range of services, there comes a point when it is necessary for a college to seek expert assistance from the local community. If, because of their very special needs, one or two students claim a disproportionate amount of time, the majority of students will have to accept only limited access to student services. Hence the need for referral. Contact with the educational psychologist or specialist medical services is best restricted to a particular member of staff, such as the head of student services. It would not be right for individual tutors to make unco-ordinated demands upon outside agencies.

Closer to hand but more difficult to co-ordinate is the relationship between LEA careers officers and college staff involved in vocational guidance. Lack of co-ordination results in duplication of effort, unequal work loads and uncertainty among staff and students. Consultation should produce a programme in which the various partners undertake activities most suited to them. Thus, a careers officer may begin by explaining to a group of students the operation of a computer-based guidance system, which is able to relate aptitudes and abilities to a range of occupations. In individual interviews afterwards, the careers officer goes through the computer printout with the aim of encouraging students to embark upon their own enquiries. At this point, a tutor can take over by giving time to listen, occasionally to probe the suitability of proposals and if need be, to stimulate fresh lines of enquiry so as to maintain momentum. From time to time, questions arise which neither tutor nor student can answer without reference to the students services unit. A well-equipped careers library (with computers to hand) provides access to up-to-date information. Sometimes, an enquiry is best dealt with by putting a student in contact with an employer for discussion, work shadowing or work experience. It will fall to the tutor to keep an eye on deadlines for applications and to assist in the preparation of references. A little later, student services may offer 'mock' interviews. And so the process continues.

What goes on in the imagination of young people as they conjure up the prospects of college from the familiar surroundings of school may bear comparison with elements drawn from Greek tragedy and Hollywood soap opera; a bit daunting perhaps, but on closer inspection attractive. They take note of the relaxed, informal atmosphere, an absence of restrictive regulations and gradually become aware of the more extensive opportunities and facilities. And yet, they feel uncertain. Size and complexity take time to assimilate.

Induction is not merely an acclimatisation of the ethos and expectations of a different institution. The more demanding part has to do with educational guidance, which begins with an assessment of a student's present situation before moving onto a survey of future possibilities. In the first term of the academic year college admissions staff visit schools to talk with fifth year pupils and parents. General information gives place to detailed discussion on courses. Sections of the college welcome school visitors. Before local careers officers begin individual interviews with fifth-formers, they and their careers colleagues in school are invited to college to learn about changes made to the programme of courses since the previous year. In this way, advice given to school pupils is as accurate and consistent as possible.

During the spring term, interviews of potential students take place; sometimes more than one interview is necessary before the right answer emerges. After the publication of summer examination results, a student's course is confirmed or modified in a further interview. A period of induction and enrolment follows (lasting one day or several), when students receive timetables for their new course and deal with matters that help produce a smooth start to the new term. Increasingly, vocational courses set aside the first few days of term for a period of orientation, so that students begin to come to terms with new styles of learning and assessment.

How does a college set about introducing potential students to full membership of its wider community? Formal events addressed by the principal are useful for explaining the college's operations and expectations. Informal tours of the college at work are popular with fifth-formers, particularly if college students act as hosts. Deeper immersion takes place during a period of induction held shortly before term begins. All new students attend. One of the first tasks is to allocate students to tutor groups, and thereafter most things are conducted on a small scale – one tutor with a manageable group of young people. Urgent though the administrative demands appear at this time, it is important to make space at the start for students to introduce themselves to one another, and the tutor to them. So much information flows during induction that certain items are lost. Some colleges distribute a handbook for students to provide a permanent record of names, maps, facilities, information about the students' union and sessional dates. Even so, not everything can be covered in a concentrated burst. The first part of term allows the process of induction to continue, both naturally and through the initiative of tutors. It makes sense to meet the careers officer or members of the students services team in a tutorial late in September rather than in a packed hall on induction day. The same thing applies to study skills; it is probable that more will be achieved with the benefit of a little student hindsight than with any amount of staff foresight.

New students will be familiar with talk of tutors and tutorials but school experience will have left its mark. An ambivalence can be detected. Whilst good relationships are very often built up between the individual pupil and tutor, it is generally true that a school tutor is responsible for a cross-section of a large number of pupils. Tutorial time is mainly taken up with activities for the whole group, and when private discussions take place, an audience of fellow pupils is close at hand. It is also part of a tutor's job to maintain standards of behaviour and enforce school regulations, not always the easiest of tasks with a group of fifth-formers. Bearing in mind the psychology of an age group close to adulthood, college managers should try to preserve the principles of good guidance whilst adapting their presentation.

In some quarters, a notion has taken hold that to be a good tutor somehow requires a special order of gifts refused to the generality of staff. No-one denies that good can be made better by training, but in the main good tutoring is only an extension of good teaching. The skills are interchangeable, the roles complementary. In some colleges all full-time staff are expected to act as tutors, although probationers may be exempted. Elsewhere, volunteers are recruited. However tutors may be appointed, young people come to value sympathetic interest and detached judgment expressed by an adult who treats them with respect. This is the heart of good tutoring.

Tutor groups vary in size from about eight to 18 students; a few are a little larger. The majority contain 12 to 14 students. In assigning students to groups, a common practice is to emphasise homogeneity so that students of similar age and course come together, tutored by a member of staff who also teaches them. In these circumstances a tutor will get to know his or her group very well. Because students share similar concerns it makes possible a closely focused tutorial programme relevant to their needs. Study skills, for example, seem to be taken more seriously when introduced in the course of classroom teaching. A tutor who happens to teach his students can extend into tutorial time the development of study skills previously touched upon in specialist class-work. Some argue, however, that close-knit groups of this kind perpetuate divisions. They discourage opportunities for personal and social development that accrue from mixing students of different ages or courses. For instance, if first and second year A level students are combined, not only is the process of familiarisation made easier for newcomers but each generation of first year students will find the path ahead already charted, possibilities as well as pitfalls. The combination of students of different ages but similar courses finds support amongst tutors, who prefer to spread administrative burdens thinly (examinations, reports, parents' evenings, references) – more doses, less pain. It could make individual interviews easier to arrange if important events like examinations and reports occur at different times for different year groups.

Other tutors dislike this arrangement on the grounds that neither half of the tutor group receives proper attention whilst the occasions for administrative action are doubled. This limited form of integration can be taken a stage further by mixing students drawn from different courses and tutored by someone who does not teach them. As an expression of what a tertiary college stands for, a place where all students are equally valued, tutor groups formed in this way will encourage unity rather than segregation amongst members of the same institution. Undoubtedly, however, much more is required of those who tutor mixed groups in terms of personal qualities as well as increased work. Staff development becomes a prerequisite.

Granted, within the framework of a common college timetable nothing but a failure of managerial will should prevent the identification of a fixed point for tutorial work. Unless this time is written in at the outset, conflicting demands (in tertiary colleges) of full-time, part-time and day-release timetables contrive to make it virtually impossible for tutors who teach their tutor groups to be free at the same time as their students. A common tutorial period allows groups to amalgamate and the expertise among staff to be shared. Communication is made easier; no small consideration in a decentralised tertiary college where students do not meet for daily registration. Brief though such encounters are, they enable the sixth form college tutors to act as messengers or investigators. Without a regular tutorial period tertiary college tutors are obliged to turn into explorers to track down their students. No tutor, however, is likely to accommodate all tutorial activity within the period or periods officially assigned. Somehow, it has a habit of overflowing into the corridor, the end of a class or the lunch queue.

Unlike tutorial periods in school, when all pupils have to be present throughout, scope for reasonable flexibility exists in post-16 colleges. It is sensible practice to require all students to be present at the start of each tutorial, if only for the most basic of reasons, i.e. to exchange information; thereafter practice can vary. Sometimes, the whole group remains or joins with other groups in activities which form part of a tutorial programme. Alternatively, a tutor may wish to see a section of students to raise issues of concern to them alone. Some of the most profitable work, however, takes place in the course of private interviews when discussion ranges over progress, difficulties and plans. The balance between working with groups and working with individual students is best left in the hands of tutors. What suits the particular style and strength of one may be seen as a straight-jacket by another. The college year has its own landmarks (or constraints), which tutors will note in the disposition of activities.

Some colleges draw up a programme of tutorial activities to include study skills, careers guidance and personal and social development. Certain items are reserved for particular times of the year, but for the rest tutors are left free to choose when and how to deal with topics. Materials will have been prepared in advance; in some cases a variety of materials to suit the approaches of different tutors. A carefully worked out syllabus may appeal to some tastes but it will operate inflexibly if it ignores those things that students perceive as important. No matter how good a programme appears at the outset it will benefit from subsequent evaluation by students no less than by staff.

Tutors of day, block-release or adult students cast themselves in the role of Cinderellas compared with colleagues who tutor full-time groups. Commonly, a tutor has responsibility for more than one group (and sometimes as many as four groups) of part-time students. In recognition of what has to be done a tutor receives a small allowance of time, which for day-release students is seldom timetabled as a tutorial period. The situation is justified by an already overcrowded day and a reluctance among certain employers to recognise the importance of tutorial work. As a result, necessary administrative tasks have to be squeezed into teaching time, or dealt with in the lecturer's own time. If a student faces problems in college or in the work place, the tutor may never find out.

Fortunately, guidance and personal development are items being pushed higher up the agenda of vocational training. For the present, a modest way forward is to provide for each part-time group a short space (15 minutes perhaps for a day-release class) when tutor and student meet to take stock of progress at college and in the work place. A brief tutorial placed at the start or finish of a day could save valuable teaching time, now vulnerable to interruption, and improve the quality of commitment and performance all round.

Adults need support too. Evening class prospectuses bring enquiries; publicity about open learning does the same. Telephone calls should be logged and passed to the appropriate member of staff, who will advise adults on the opportunities and modes of attendance available in their part of the college. Once enrolled, the part-time student may turn to his original adviser in the same way that a full-time student might turn to a tutor.

Once the spotlight beams down on the tutorial work – usually, it is true, with the aim of enhancing its importance – doubting voices will be heard off-stage. Students have survived well enough up till now without the apparatus of a nanny state. Extra tutorial time will merely lead to the creation of artificial activities, for which staff have neither training nor sympathy. Against these murmurings the argument for tutoring has to be won. Fundamentally, it rests its case on helping students define and achieve their educational goals. When it comes to matters of practice, it may help to establish a foundation of essential responsibilities best determined after wide consultation. These become matters which all tutors must cover: transmission of information and essential administrative tasks; liaison with other members of staff who teach their students; checks on students' attendance and progress, including written reports; oversight of vocational guidance; and contact with parents. Beyond these tasks (or whatever are defined as central responsibilities of a tutor), there is scope for some diversity of practice that takes account of preferred styles of working among staff and the wide spectrum of needs among students.

If tutors claim to be finding their way through unfamiliar territory, someone must provide signposts. In one direction, it can be a matter of resources – a catalogue of accessible materials augmented by teachers' notes. Some colleges provide tutors with packs of resources at the start of a new year. At one college, a tutorial support group, consisting of interested tutors, decided to issue a termly magazine designed to share workable ideas and elicit a response from tutors. No attempt was made to enforce a particular style of tutoring. Tutors were free to select as little or as much as they wanted. Alongside this work, the tutorial support group conducted a college-wide survey of tutors of part-time groups, which revealed a variety of practice and identified areas for action.

Another initiative produced a self-appraisal booklet to help A level students set themselves targets for periodic review with their tutors. A staff meeting time, fixed at some point during the working day, enables tutors to meet at regular intervals to transact business and to engage in that most effective form of in-service training, namely the sharing of good practice among fellow practitioners. A forum like this allows for the generation of steam as well as inspiration, which is no bad thing if irritations disappear on ventilation. Days set aside for college-wide in-service training can be used to introduce the contribution of specialists, through workshops in basic counselling skills, health education, higher educational guidance or profiling. As confidence and experience increase, staff may come closer to agreement about what constitutes the repertoire of a good teacher. For the present, it has to be said that blessed harmony exists only among the spheres.

What of the future? An outline of things to come already appears on the horizon; indeed for some, colleges may have become a present reality. As TVEI extends its way into every college, all students up to the age of 18 will be drawn under its influence. TVEI enlarges the role of the tutor by incorporating vocational guidance within the broad domain of personal guidance. Opportunities for regular formative assessment have to be included within a student's programme, culminating in the compilation of a final record of achievement. The person to whom this process of guidance most naturally falls (given training and time) must be the tutor. Increasingly, college administrators will turn to tutors to provide them with basic data for student information systems as a preliminary to the wider activity of decision-making and future planning of colleges and LEAs. No more backs of envelopes for record-keeping in the late 20th-century world of high technology.

6 Liaison in post-16 education – an essential ingredient

Peter Lineham

The case for liaison

Until well into the 1960s education in England and Wales seemed set in its 'top down' form, with primary schools unduly influenced (through the 11+) by the secondary sector, and with the curriculum and examinations in secondary schools dominated by the demands of higher education, to which only a small minority would proceed. Such liaison as there was between institutions consisted, therefore, of the 'junior' ascertaining the demands of the 'senior', a situation largely accepted by all concerned.

Schools did, of course, liaise with parents, but this was usually limited to discussion of academic progress once a year, unless they were unlucky enough to be called to account for some misconduct by their progeny. Liaison with employers varied greatly; at a time when school leavers had comparatively little difficulty in finding jobs there were secondary-modern schools who nevertheless took employer liaison seriously, whereas too many selective schools regarded those who did not proceed to higher education as having 'failed'.

Whatever liaison there may have been in the 'vertical' (primary-secondary secondary-higher education or second-ary-employment) mode, no need was perceived for 'lateral' liaison; indeed, in many cases, schools (both primary and secondary) were in competition with each other, especially at the 11+ and 18+ points. Both headteachers and assistants rarely met colleagues from other schools, unless they were active in professional associations. Only with the advent of the Certificate of Secondary Education were teachers from groups of schools thrown together in professional engagement and even then, the selective sector was not involved for a long time. Often, too, the stimulus to meet was perceived as external and distant, despite the requirement for local moderation meetings, and many teachers revealed their conditioning by opting for the mode of examining which demanded least participation from them.

The beginnings of change

These observations are made simply least we forget the changes which comprehensive education in general, and the growth of tertiary and sixth form colleges in particular, have brought about. Primary education has been allowed and encouraged to develop, secondary schools have been compelled – by reorganisation, by moves towards a national curriculum, by changes in forms of examination, by shrinking job opportunities and by the operation of the Manpower Services Commission – to be more outward-looking; and the 16–19 colleges have been creating their new roles. Even higher education has shown some signs of change, although it would not be difficult to argue a case that too many of its institutions wish to maintain the status quo ante where all liaison was upward.

The advent of tertiary education

It is the tertiary sector development which, because it emphasises virtues of a break at 16+ with its attendant educational and employment reorientation, has caused the most radically involved parties to rethink their liaison. For simplicity's sake, it is proposed to use the term 'tertiary' to describe all colleges dealing exclusively with students after the end of compulsory education at 16+; so that, not only true tertiary colleges but also sixth form colleges and those colleges of further education which have little, if any, post-19 work are included. There is no such thing as a free-standing tertiary system in education – it only exists as the third phase after primary and secondary, and before the fourth, higher education. Nevertheless, the tertiary sector is of particular importance, looking both ways as it does – backwards into secondary education (especially in its last two years) and forwards into work or higher education. It stands at the point where young people leave compulsory education and begin to exercise choice over the direction in which they would like to go. In order to be effective a tertiary college must continuously expose itself to all kinds of influence, within and without education. It must also be prepared to influence others (fellow educationists and those in industry and commerce) in the interests of the young people it serves.

A new kind of liaison

In such a system, where students are faced with crucial choices but are perhaps in the college for only one year (more usually two and at the most three), it is no longer tolerable that schools and colleges remain moated castles, isolated both from each other and from industry and commerce, as microcosms of the individual teachers in their 'private' classrooms. The informal and partial, sometimes almost non-existent, contacts of the past must be replaced by formal systems, specifically designed to assist the education and inform the choices of students.

There is also a need for such systems in the sixth forms of 11–18 schools, a need which is not so readily perceived because of the internal move of the students from pre- to post-compulsory education and the assumptions made about the schools' (often limited) provision. However, it will be clearer if the example of one post-16 college, or a set of colleges which provide for the majority of those who continue their education after the compulsory period, is used.

Partnership

The way we use language frequently reveals our attitudes, and it is not without significance that contributory schools have become partner schools. Where tertiary colleges are providing most of the area's post-16 education and training, liaison systems based on this partnership have developed; one should not underestimate the degree of rethinking and change of attitudes that this has required. Nor must it be forgotten that a partnership needs to be formed with the student – the day of packaged advice, handed out with a minimum of discussion, is past. The 16 year-old may be limited in experience, his self-knowledge not far enough advanced, yet he has to make a decision about what to do next. No matter how much information, guidance, stimulus or pressure he may receive, the final choice is his – even when it does not appear to be – and he has to live with its consequences. If we forget that all liaison is about partnership between the student and the education system set up to serve him, we shall fail.

Managerial liaison

Good management in education has never been more important and, in a system where responsibilities for the student as he moves through it is shared by several institutions, it is essential that there should be liaison and partnership between the heads and principals involved; and between those managers and the LEA to whom they are immediately responsible. The most promising mechanism for co-operation seems to be the area board, known as the board of studies. It is essential that such a board should be formally constituted, that all heads and principles from the area should be personally involved and that the LEA be represented. Without such formality and an agreed consti-tution, there is considerable danger that the many pressures on institutions will first fragment and then destroy the system – there has to be commitment.

Once those who manage the secondary and tertiary institutions of an area begin to meet regularly, their mutual concerns will generate more than enough for each agenda; indeed, one of the main functions of such a group may well be discussion of, and the allocating priorities between, the many internally arising concerns and externally imposed initiatives. Anyone who has served on such a board (at least two boards have now been in existence for more than 15 years) will testify to the way in which their perceptions have been sharpened and their preconceptions challenged. Two main areas of work tend to predominate; the first being curriculum, which includes responses to initiatives from government and from examination boards; the second, policy and administration vis-à-vis the LEA, whether in its domestic role or as the agent of central government. Rather than deal in generalities, it may be more informative to show how one of the boards mentioned above has recently been dealing with curriculum, and how it sees its role in relation to the LEA, together with a note of a typical term's agendas and some remarks about the tension (constructive if properly managed) between the collective operation of the board and autonomy of the institutions. In curricular matters, there is both a frank exchange of information about how each school organises its curriculum in general and consideration of particular areas of concern. For instance, one complete session was set aside for each head in order to set out the philosophy and proposed operation of his future fourth and fifth year curriculum, with special reference to pre-vocational developments. The questioning and discussion was illuminating; it clearly caused heads to scrutinise their proposals more rigorously and constructively than was likely to be possible during internal debate. This extra dimension of a debate of future plans with peers was clearly thought to be of value. As an example of a particular curricular concern, the board has been, over a period, locked in a struggle with the problems of core science and with the lack of progress in the local Secondary Schools Science Review group.

Although debate has been vigorous and criticism uninhibited, this has not been simply a matter of talking shop – a sub-group of the board is now working up a proposal for a core science programme to be adopted throughout the area.

The post-16 curriculum is also subjected to scrutiny, particularly that offered by the college (there are two 11–18 schools on the board), which not only admits 80% of all those continuing full-time education beyond 16 but provides all traditional part-time training in the area, including off-the-job training for the great majority of the people on the Youth Training Scheme. Schools are rightly concerned that those with whom they have been involved for five years should be properly catered for, and the board provides a forum at which sharp questioning of the college can be directed. As well as the extensive information and consultation programme organised for all fifth formers in the area, there are four visits to the college for school staff each year; members of the board feel that it is essential to maintain this open approach. The two 11–18 schools are not so open because they retain a proportion of their fifth formers in the sixth forms but, because all post-16 matters are properly seen as the board's concern, their sixth form provision is scrutinised in a way that does not occur in other school sixth forms.

The board also addresses itself to matters of policy and administration vis-à-vis the LEA. Two benefits accrue: a forum created where frank and open discussion of issues both reduces the isolation of the individual manager (head or principal) and allows a balanced view to prevail, and, when a common view on an important issue emerges at board level, members can represent it collectively to the LEA with all the weight of those who manage 11–19 education across a whole area. Matters recently dealt with have included staffing levels in a falling roll situation, the shortcomings of the Schools' Psychological Service, in-service training for teaching and non-teaching staff and the effects of industrial action.

The following selection from topics dealt with in a recent autumn term may give some idea of the actual operation of the board:

- Discussion of the chairman's draft annual report and the agenda for the meeting with the Chief Education Officer;
- review of courses for very able pupils in science, modern languages and art and design;
- review of summer public examination results (schools and colleges);

- GCSE and its implications for the future of the 11–16 curriculum;
- college finance;
- admission of the press to governors' meetings;
- liaison with Association of Secondary Heads;
- JTIGCAL (careers guidance) pilot scheme;
- in-service for heads of department;
- interface at 16+ with post–16 education, training, employment and unemployment;
- update on music festival;
- higher level INSET for, and secondment of staff;
- arrangements for meetings between the board and teachers' centre wardens;
- curriculum 14–19, especially co-operation with SSCR and GCSE groups.

It is essential to be clear-eyed about the limitations of a board. It cannot relieve an individual head or principal of either his autonomy or the responsibility which goes with it. This may be recognised by the avoidance of voting – if there is no unanimity, individuals are left to disagree and act as they feel they must. Paradoxically, this freedom is an incentive to agreement rather than a licence to do one's own thing. Heads and principals also have an allegiance to governors, and it is essential that governors understand the board and its functions. Consideration might well be given to the practice of one of the boards of long standing, where chairmen and vice-chairmen of governors meet the board from time to time for an exchange of information and views.

One undeniable benefit of a board is the stimulus it gives its members towards professional growth. It is very difficult to remain parochial when regularly confronted with what is going on elsewhere in the area, and having to expose one's views and practices to the scrutiny and criticism of others. Debate is frank, not infrequently heated, but mixed with humour and goodwill, and is always directed towards consensus about the principles and best method of education for the young people of the area. There are many who would testify to the support the board gave them when they were newly appointed and the opportunity it has provided since to sharpen their wits and improve their practice.

Liaison between teachers

Managerial liaison will never be effective if those who organise and direct students' learning are not involved; no-one with any experience will think this is other than very difficult, but it must happen. There are several levels of operation.

The first level is within the school department or college section. Without going into detail, it has to be said that, unless teachers are encouraged to be open with each other and co-operate at the subject level, there is little chance of progress on wider curriculum issues.

The next level is where heads of department or section are involved with each other, either within a faculty framework or, more usually, in discussion over the the whole curriculum under the chairmanship of senior management. There are manifold pressures on these important subject managers to co-operate only with reluctance and to be suspicious of change; anyone who has participated in a discussion of 'whole curriculum', at either a school heads of department meeting or a college academic board, needs no convincing of this unfortunate fact. The subject-based curriculum and the system of teacher-training which first served and now perpetuates it, militate against open-minded discussion and forward-looking decison-making, not least because the promotion and rewarding of teachers is bound up with them. Teachers feel that they are competent only within a quite closely circumscribed curriculum area; they are called to account if results in that area are not good, and are therefore (understandably) reluctant to move into new areas or yield class-time or resources which 'their' subject 'needs'.

This makes the next level of liaison, between teachers from various schools and colleges, even more hazardous. There should be little doubt that this kind of liaison is profitable, yet, if it is not most carefully set up and managed it is doomed to failure. Even if the obstacles of timing, industrial action and cover for absence are overcome, whoever organises the meetings has to have clear objectives, must fully inform participants of them and must convince teachers that the work will be productive. Meetings alone will not do – visits to each other's schools or colleges and visits to places outside the immediate area should figure in the programme. It is worth repeating here that, where staff from colleges are involved with colleagues from partner schools, 'top down' attitudes must be avoided; certain external requirements have to be taken into account (e.g. national entry standards to certain courses), but these should not be used indiscriminately in this connection – it is a fact that most teachers in schools know much less than college colleagues about the ethos and range of work undertaken in the latter's institution; it follows that, even though reciprocal visits are desirable, regular opportunities for school staff to visit the college(s), to which many of their young people proceed, is a priority. The particular relevance of inter-institutional teacher contact will be mentioned when student/parent guidance is considered.

The greater capacity of an area board to respond constructively to external initiatives and pressures has already been mentioned, and what is true of managers is also true of teachers. Schools will always vary in teacher and managerial expertise and in resources, so their final responses will be different. Nevertheless, if the teachers of an area can meet, under the aegis of an area board, to discuss how best to respond and to develop schemes, at the very least, they will feel less isolated and thus better able to cope; at best, they may well develop (with the help of LEA advisers) strategies which would otherwise not have occurred to them as being feasible, within their competence or within their resources.

Liaison at 16 +

It is worth risking the charge of piety to say again that the student is the only reason for the existence of schools and colleges; it needs reiteration, because institutions and their staffs develop a rationale of their own which can diminish the importance of the student and relegate him, in extreme cases, to the status of a pawn. It is not that teachers do not care about those in their charge but that they are subtly affected by pressures such as external examinations, their own prospects and, not infrequently, threats to the survival of their school or college. It seems necessary to be frank about such matters when considering liaison at 16+, when grave decisions have to be made and when the self-interest of institutions is a factor not to be neglected.

It goes without saying that the 14–16 years in schools must be a period when students are encouraged and helped to work more through self-direction than in earlier years, and this is part of the process by which responsibility is taken for the first really important decision in life – what to do at 16+. Like any other decision, this must be based on full, accurate and unbiased information, and this is where first-class liaison procedures and the elimination (so far as possible) of the self-interest of institutions are of crucial importance. Parental involvement is, as always, necessary, and the same information must be provided for parents as for students so that they may fully understand the alternatives.

All this demands a degree of co-operation between institutions which has never before existed. Take first the case of a sole provider post-16 college – in other words, a true tertiary college – which operates in an area with a number of partner schools. An information and consultation programme can readily be set up, which affords both students and parents direct access in their own schools to college staff, to careers service staff and to employers and Youth Training Scheme providers; the latter two are less easy to organise but must be included. The area board is the obvious body to set up and monitor this operation.

It is more likely that there will be several post-16 providers; there may be 11–18 schools in the local system and there may be more than one type of post-16 college, sixth form or FE. In this case there will be competition, and it is foolish not to recognise the fact, but it is possible for that competition to operate to the advantage of students. Although it may involve a long and costly process of liaison, each student can be given the chance to make the choice to which he is entitled by eliminating most of the bias inherent in a divided system. There are two essential ingredients in this process; one is the existence of an area board, where those who manage the various institutions may get to know each other and move towards co-operative and complementary provision; the other is the realisation by all concerned that a dragooned or misled student is likely to be a poor student. These processes of liaison and co-operation imply changes in that which institutions offer and demand that courses be seen as answering student needs, not as receptacles which must be filled by a sufficient number of bodies each year. Nobody underestimates what this kind of co-operative policy means for individual institutions; they will be assailed by disturbing changes and, in some cases, by threats to their very survival. Nevertheless, there is no case at all for deliberate withholding of liaison and co-operation.

Teachers are reluctant to complete forms. In one sense this is laudable, since most forms have faults; some are so ill-thought out and open-ended as to elicit either a massive essay or half-a-dozen meaningless words, others are so tightly structured as to frustrate the teacher who wants to communicate more fully and subtly – although this type does compel a response from the lazy and the uninterested. Despite these drawbacks, documentation is necessary, and there can be a compromise between the kinds of form caricatured above. However, if the goodwill of teachers is to be gained and maintained it is important that they should not be asked to complete a whole series of forms for different users and, furthermore, they are entitled to assurance that the effort and time they devote results in a document which is taken seriously by the end-user, and is thus of benefit to the student.

Once again, co-operation through an area board will make for efficiency. It is possible to design a form which will combine the recording of factual data about a 16+ student with forecasts of academic attainment and opinions about attitudes and ability to cope with continuing education and employment; the latter are clearly only opinions, and their validity will be affected by the quality of the relationships between institutions and the way in which such information and opinions are used. Great care has to be taken over the design of this kind of documentation; both generators and users have to be consulted and, even when a satisfactory document emerges, all must keep reminding themselves that it is only a basis for communication between student, parents, school staff, careers officers and the staff of post-16 institutions. Modern technology, even if only at the level of no-carbon-required paper, allows multi-use without the teacher having to complete different forms for different users.

The kind of information and guidance document just referred to is probably not suitable for employers in its entirety. Employers vary so widely, in the kind of information they want, the qualities they look for in applicants, their ability to interpret teachers' forecasts and opinions, and in the amount of time they are prepared to devote to selection, that it is likely to be in the student's interests that the school should use information and opinions contained in the basic form to respond to the individual employer. This is where long-term relationships, cultivated assiduously over many years by schools and colleges with, at least, the major employers of the area, pay tangible dividends for students seeking employment; as between partner school and post-16 colleges, so between schools/colleges and employers, mutual trust in quality of information and validity of opinions must be built up and maintained.

Parents will, in a well-organised school, have become even more involved in discussion as their children approach the 16+ decision. Attitudes will vary, from the parent who says 'I just want her to do what she wants', to the one who actually completes the application form and appears at the college ready to try to dominate the discussion. Both want the best for their children and both have a most important contribution to make; they know things about their children and their capacities which no-one else knows. Nevertheless, the process of liaison should allow parents to gain a realistic view of their children's ability, to meet the demands of employment or continuing education; over-estimation is more common, not unnaturally, but under-estimation also occurs. The process of liaison at 16+, therefore, must include meetings with parents, en masse and individually, usually with, but sometimes without, their children; and it may justly be claimed that, in a well-designed and humanely-administered system, greater understanding between parents and children is an important by-product. Certainly, where continuing education is an option, a programme carefully orchestrated by school and post-16 college(s) can be of enormous benefit to students and their parents, even if the former end up employed or on a YTS scheme, simply because they will have considered the education options seriously and rejected them in favour of work or a training scheme; positive rejection is in many ways as valuable as acceptance.

Liaison with higher education

Although this affects only a minority of the whole pre-16 population of a school, probably not more than 40% of those continuing after 16, it is something which has to be seriously addressed in any post-16 college. There are a number of obvious difficulties here; colleges vary greatly in what they provide, they are mostly some hundreds of miles distant, they are too often wedded to a top-down view of education and dictate entry requirements in a way appearing draconian to applicants, and the vast majority work through the necessarily complex apparatus of either the Universities Central Council for Admissions or the Polytechnics Central Admissions Service. Time is also a factor – students have to begin to prepare for their application to higher education after only about six months of a two-year course; they are compelled (in most cases) to complete their decision-making within about fifteen months of having entered the post-16 college.

For those who aspire to Oxbridge, the programme of application and interview starts even earlier.

The first requirement to help students in a post-16 college cope with the complexities of seeking a place in higher education (or, indeed, a post in employment) is the appointment of staff who will keep up-to-date with the enormous amount of factual information and with the ever-changing requirements and procedures of universities, polytechnics, colleges of education, colleges of higher education, colleges of music, art and drama and other specialist institutions, as well as those of the fields of employment into which the courses may lead. The scale of staffing will vary according to college size, but an absolute minimum is an academic member of staff (with an appropriate background, qualifications and training), with a no greater than half-time teaching commitment, and a non-teaching full-time member who will manage the clerical, library and administrative aspects of the work. The latter is an anchor post which will demand skill, devotion, tact and a sympathy with and understanding of young people, as well as a knowledge of the system they are confronting; luckily, there are suitable people if one looks hard enough, but unluckily, it is very difficult to pay them what they are worth. Needless to say, suitable accommodation must be found which will allow storage and display of prospectuses and other information and which will afford privacy for consultations and interviews, not only with college staff and by careers service staff (with whom close liaison is vital) but with visiting specialists, such as those from the armed services, nursing or specialist industries.

It will be necessary to set up programmes assisting students in their choice of higher education, and these will need to start in the second term of a two-year course. A possible pattern will begin with an introduction to the opportunities available, with an overview of the college's programme and information about what resources are available and where they may be found; a published schedule of timings is vital at this point. The next stage will probably include some form of contact with personalities from higher education, and the third stage (in the later third and early fourth terms) will be a carefully managed and monitored period of hard decision-making and application. The fourth stage will consist of monitoring responses throughout the late fourth and fifth terms, and the last stage will occur in the summer when public examination results are known and final decisions are made. In a medium-sized tertiary college of about 1200 full-time students, there are likely to be about 350 students considering courses in higher education (from Higher National Diploma upwards) or, of course, equivalent employment, so that the annual exercise described above is a considerable undertaking.

Given the wide dispersion of institutions and the different attitudes and standards among any one institution's various departments, making personal contact is very difficult. However, there are two ways in which a carefully organised college programme can put some flesh on the bare bones of prospectuses, degree course guides and other literature. Students should be encouraged to visit the institutions on their short list, either on their own, with parents or with college staff; always bearing in mind that seeing the physical stituation alone can be as unhelpful and misinforming as cold print; every attempt should be made on such visits to meet students (preferably of the target department faculty) who are often willing to talk with visitors and show them something of the place. The other way of arranging contact is to bring higher education staff to the tertiary college; where there is an audience of 300+ students, it is quite feasible to invite about 25 staff from universities, polytechnics and other colleges. Careful selection can give contact with a range of disciplines so as to afford students something more than generalisations, and it is wise also to include representatives from any major areas of employment interest. While students at 18+ must be encouraged, even more than at 16+, to be responsible for their own decisions, parents are involved emotionally and financially, and the college must try to keep them informed so that the dialogue between them and their children may be constructive.

One way of doing this is to hold an HE evening, to which two or three HE staff are invited, first to talk briefly (especially about the variations and hazards of selection and admission) and to take part in a structured discussion. Careful organisation (with previous circulation of factual summaries of procedures and time-schedules) and firm chairmanship are essential to the success of this venture. At worst, this operation may clear up misunderstandings and partially allay fears; at best, it may foster better understanding and positive co-operation between parents and children at a time which is a great strain for them all.

Liaison with the local community and within the college

The very existence of a large post-16 institution, especially in a medium-sized or small town, is a significant feature in the landscape; such a college will be the principal centre, perhaps in an area 50 miles in diameter, not only for full-time post-16 education but for every kind of part-time study and training. On any one day, there will be students attending full-time courses of every complexion from the wholly academic to those with a very large vocational element (block-release and day-release students sent by their employers, students on every kind of Youth Training Scheme doing off-the-job training, or life-skills education business people and industrialists attending one-or two-day seminars, and other adults making use of facilities and expertise for leisure purposes).

This situation demands that the principal, the vice-principals and heads of department of the college spend time and energy making and maintaining every kind of contact with local industry and business, with local government, with statutory and voluntary bodies, with the police and with the press. It is possible to achieve this, in part, by the creation of such bodies as advisory committees for aspects of the college's work such as business, catering, construction and enginerering; if well-run, these can be agents both for preventing the college becoming too detached from commercial and industrial realities and for stimulating employers with fresh ideas and widening their horizons, and the result should be better-trained and more efficient employees. Nevertheless, these activities are limited in scope: the effectiveness of a college and its right to be a force in the community will depend on the vigour and efficiency with which it carries out its educational function and on the quality of the personal relationships between all its staff and the individuals who make up that community. A prime task of senior management is to ensure, not least by personal example, that the college is seen to have a human face and to act as a helping agency; lack of flexibility and any trace of 'holier-than-thou' will disable it. However energetic and efficient senior staff are in contacts with the community, it is the way in which the individual teacher, librarian, receptionist, secretary, college nurse, cleaner or caretaker responds to students (of any age) which leaves the deepest impressions; hence this linking of community and internal college liaison. There are, of course, formal arrangements built into the constitutions of colleges, such as the Governing Body and the Academic Board; these can be dealt with briefly before returning to the wider and less formal liaison. As at present constituted, governing bodies tend to be less effective than they could be; political considerations can and do distort their representation of the educational interests of the local community, and there are still too many governors who have little understanding of the processes of education in general and the operation of their own college in particular. However, there are, fortunately, many who are full of goodwill and eager to learn; they often bring a variety of expertise to the (somewhat infrequent) meetings and are willing to fight for their college at district council and LEA levels. Good liaison is essential between the principal and an active chairman of governors; apart from having a crucial role in the field of appointments, a wise chairman who supports and encourages (and, on occasions, cautions) the principal is a jewel beyond price. But liaison should not be the private preserve of principals, vice-pricipals and chairmen; opportunities must be used (and created, if necessary) for heads of department to meet and to work with chairmen, vice-chairmen and other leading governors.

The other statutory instrument of liaison, the college academic board, depends for its effectiveness on the view of it taken by its main constituent members. It usually consists of equal numbers of ex-officio members (principal, vice-principals, heads of department and chief administrative officer) and elected members chosen from teaching and administrative staff across the college; some boards will also have representation from the area liaison board. In a sense, everything depends on the principal who chairs – if he/she is a listener who is truly open to others' views there will be profitable debate resulting in agreed (or, at any rate, understood) action, but if he/she is determined to be autocratic, then it is possible that genuine debate will be stifled and that members may be denied a voice in the management of the college. It should, however, be said that the effectiveness of a board does not depend on a principal. It also turns on the willingness of the board as a whole (and of its elected members in particular) to accept executive functions, and to be accountable for the way they carry them out. In some colleges, for instance, the finance and staffing sub-committees of the board determine policy and take decisions, subject only to the veto of the principal who remains the only statutorily accountable officer. Some colleges have an ethos which encourages a principal to share powers and responsibilities in this way, and gives elected members confidence to accept that privilege and burden; other colleges, either because of the way they have developed or because of the personalities of the managers and elected members, shy away from the delegation model and are of the opinion that 'they are paid to manage – let them manage and accept praise (perhaps!) if it goes right and blame (certainly!) if it goes wrong'. One thing is certain, academic boards need sensitive handling if they are to be the effective instruments into which they can develop. The regard in which a community holds its local college will, in the last analysis, depend not on governing bodies or academic boards but on the personal experiences which students and their parents have in their contacts with it. Yet, it is the ethos of the college, created by the style of management, which most of all conditions the way in which staff treat those that it exists to serve, and the ways in which personal and professional relationships are handled by both management and staff determine the health of the institution. It seems unfortunate that some people working in education perceive a dichotomy between efficiency and charisma; we could all cite examples of the extreme view – the caring teacher who despises 'administration' or the dedicated manager who has no time for 'sloppiness' – but it is a fact that those who are most effective in education are both efficient and charismatic. If an institution has sufficient of these people at all levels it will be 'healthy' and will appear so to the community it serves.

Conclusion

This thesis proposes that the institutions which make up our educational system cannot function properly, as most did in the past, as isolated units. The increasing complexity of society's demands on education make liaison essential; the degree will vary but, at the very least, there must be both knowledge of what others are doing and strong links with the community served. More time, effort and resources are given to students when they reach the 14–18 period; liaison becomes more important than pre-14. It is a sad fact that, for a whole variety of reasons, education is suffering a crisis of confidence and this, in turn, tends to diminish public confidence in the system. There is no single solution to this difficulty, but effective liaison between institutions and especially with the whole community, where time is taken to listen to others and to explain objectives, must be an essential ingredient in the mix of measures needed to put matters right.

7 The curriculum and its delivery

Rob Stephenson

The nature of the curriculum

Before deciding on a policy for curriculum delivery, it is necessary to decide what the curriculum should be. This may seem obvious, but in practice many problems and arguments arise because different people are making different and conflicting assumptions. All too often, statements about the effectiveness of the education system or about individual schools or colleges are made on the basis of false assumptions about the curriculum, which have not been thought through. It is, therefore, necessary to start with a careful consideration of the curriculum itself.

1. What areas of activity have a legitimate claim to be included?
2. Should the curriculum be the same for all students in the age group?
3. If not, what should be included for which groups?

The curriculum is the means of achieving all the 'aims' of an institution. It includes all activities which are intended to provide experiences and which, at the same time, fall within the broad meaning of education.

Education is about preparing young people for the achievement of their full potential in all aspects of adult life. Therefore a full educational curriculum should include personal development as well as intellectual and skill development. Within intellectual and skill development, the curriculum should include the fostering of all abilities, skills and aptitudes that will contribute to a full, active and satisfying life. It will include an element of socialisation, but should not be indoctrination. It will incorporate preparation for the world of work, because, for the majority of the population, work will be a major part of adult life. However, the emphasis of an educational curriculum should be on the growth and fulfilment of potential for the individual rather than the production, to order, of certain kinds of employment applicants.

If an institution wishes consciously and deliberately to produce sensible, responsible, caring, thinking, mature young people who have the personal skills needed to work effectively in a team; who will take a responsible, co-operative, yet constructively critical role in either an organisation or a community; who can make satisfying, healthy and constructive use of leisure time; and who will contribute to an optimisation of the quality of life for themselves and for those around them; then that institution must give priority to personal as well as intellectual development in its curriculum.

The curriculum encompasses the whole of an institution's mode of operation and all of its activities. Some parts of the curriculum will be formally timetabled, other parts will not, but this does not mean that they are less important. The term 'extra-curricular' activities is misleading. In many colleges and schools, 'non-timetabled' activities are very much a part of the quality of provision and should, therefore, be regarded as a part of the curriculum. The alternative term, 'hidden curriculum', is even more misleading. Valuable non-time-tabled activities should not be hidden, they should be kept in the forefront of the consciousness of everyone who is involved in the delivery of the curriculum; such activities should be recognised and supported. Better descriptions of this kind of objective and activity are the 'non-timetabled curriculum', the 'indirect curriculum' or the 'informal curriculum'. Use of such terms would allow us to recognise explicitly what everyone knows, namely that there are some educational communities, schools and colleges, which are highly regarded because of the influence of the informal curriculum, just as much as, if not more than, of the formal, timetabled curriculum.

Within the formal or timetabled curriculum, there are two aspects which should be distinguished. The one can be described as the process and outcomes of education, the other is the vehicle or means of education. It is the latter which includes the factual material or specific skills and ideas that are too frequently regarded as the sole content of the curriculum. It is important, before considering what might be the best method of delivery, to be clear about the relative importance to be attached to content, as regards specific knowledge and specific skills, and, on the other hand, to outcomes, in the sense of the growth of generalised personal qualities which will be developed through the vehicle of the content.

The curriculum includes both the criteria by which any set of activities can be included within the education provided by a college, and also the list of activities themselves. The criteria themselves will include two groups, those that characterise outcomes and those that characterise processes by means of which people gradually become educated.

It is also important to distinguish between educational aims and training objectives, and to determine their relative priorities. There is no doubt that education and training are inseparable in that training in certain skills, such as reading, is a prerequisite of education. Training beyond the most basic, will, conversely, be constrained, limited and inhuman if not accompanied by genuine education. Education means 'the strengthening of the powers of body and mind'. Training is 'preparation for performance by instruction, practice and drill'. The balance of importance between process and content will differ between a full educational curriculum and a training course.

Historical background – two traditions

Attitudes to the curriculum contain one or both of two discernible threads emanating from separate historical backgrounds and traditions, which have, until recently, been converging but which are, perhaps, now diverging.

The one tradition derives from the liberal education provided in the universities and ancient schools, continued in the direct-grant, independent and grammar schools, and now central to the work of some comprehensive schools and some colleges. In this liberal, educational tradition, process is at least as important as content; the 'Aims' stress the strengthening of the powers of mind and body, and all participants share and actively work for the common values, standards and priorities of the institution. It is a feature of this tradition that process, outcomes and generalised skill development are more important than subject content itself. Indeed, subject content is seen primarily as a vehicle for personal and intellectual development, and the first criterion for choice of subject content is its effectiveness in this respect. It must be accepted that in its worst manifestations, this tradition has lost its way and it can become little more than a knee-jerking suppliant to narrow academia, with more regard for protection of the purity or 'popularity' of subject discipline than for the growth of the powers of mind and body of the student. Fortunately, however, this caricature does not generally reflect the truth in colleges. Recent developments have added a second priority in the selection of subject content within this tradition. This is relevant to the modern world and to the world of employment. The liberal education tradition is alive and well. It is a strong feature of sixth form and genuine tertiary colleges, and is probably the main feature in recognition of 'good' colleges by students, by parents and by employers and higher education.

The second tradition derives from publicly provided, centrally and politically controlled, 'prolonged elementary schooling', linked with post-school technical, commercial and trade training. It is associated with socialisation for compliance, vocational training of the narrow job-preparation style, and technical training in which the driving force is employers' needs. At its best, this tradition includes a very high degree of vocational relevance, a good match with what was, in the past, expected of the majority of the population in adult life and, perhaps, avoids what some currently popular political philosophers would see as the danger of raising expectation levels too high or of producing an over-critical and dissatisfied population.

Through the sixties and seventies, the two traditions were

on converging courses. The idealism of the belief in comprehensive education was one of 'education for all'. It assumed the philosophy of process typical of the liberal education tradition, but sought, as the vehicle, more immediately applicable content rather than narrow academic subjects. At the same time, narrow vocational training was broadening and placing greater emphasis on broad personal skills. Liberal studies departments grew apace in technical colleges; greater emphasis was placed on 'applicable' subjects on the schools side, with the growth of A levels in such subjects as engineering science, computer studies, business and industrial studies, economics, design and electronics: Latin, Greek and syllabuses in most subjects were revised to take more account of applications.

The external background

It is impossible to predict employment opportunities for more than a very few years ahead in other than the most general terms. There are, however, certain trends in employment opportunities and manpower needs and these all indicate the following:

- The need for flexibility in employment;
- the need for breadth and strength of initial education as a foundation to train and retrain as technologies change within a working lifetime;
- the need for greater emphasis on developed intellectual and personal skills;
- a lower proportion of adult life spent at work in paid employment.

This points to the need for a highly educated population rather than an educated minority and a narrowly socialised/ trained majority. Taken to its logical conclusion, it means that the best vocational preparation for the age group is an extended general education. The future of a post-industrial economy requires that it should now apply to as large a majority of the population as possible.

And yet, recent trends in national policy and in educational policy indicate a backward move; a return towards a narrow view of vocational preparation for the majority, with education in a broad-based sense reserved for the few.

The range of curriculum opportunities available to the 16–19 age group should take account of the fact that the long term needs of society, the economy and many individual students, is for a broad educational foundation, upon which successive periods of rapid specific training can be based as employment requirements and opportunities change and fluctuate in response to changing technologies. The system should be offering a range of curriculum opportunities in full-time general education to suit the whole range of abilities and levels of achievement at the end of compulsory schooling, and should be encouraging more young people to participate particularly in this kind of provision.

The full educational curriculum is not appropriate for everyone beyond the end of compulsory schooling. A college must decide how appropriate its curriculum is to its students.

A curriculum description

The full liberal education curriculum should include the following three major elements:

1. Education for personal development.
2. General intellectual/skill development.
3. Specialist intellectual/skill development.

The major decisions about curriculum delivery thus relate to the following:

– The balance of emphasis between the elements for particular groups of students;
– the range of specialist opportunities to be provided;
– the optimum content vehicle for the delivery of general and intellectual skills;
– the style and effectiveness of delivery.

Breadth in the 16–19 curriculum

In recent years, there has been increasing unease about the narrowness of the 16–19 curriculum, but at the same time, there has been great pressure on institutions to place total priority on the specialist element, and within that, to concentrate on qualification and examination objectives where the emphasis is on content. The pressure on the post-16 curriculum has been towards employment preparation, with emphasis on content which is relevant for the early stages of employment. Many young people in the 16–19 age group have started to form clear ideas about their intended career and are ready, and indeed impatient, to specialise. This desire should not be ignored, but it does not imply that such students do no also want to continue their general education. It is, indeed, a feature of the age group to be deeply interested in broad social/economic/philosophical/political issues. The purpose behind the general education element in the curriculum should be to:

– develop a mature understanding of man's place in society and in the universe;
– give an understanding and appreciation of how the students own specialism fits into the range of human activity;
– give students an awareness of how other specialisms operate and contribute.

The general education element is not only a theory of knowledge course; it should produce an understanding and appreciation of the interelation of all human activity. It can, perhaps, be thought of as the design and the cement that holds together the bricks (specialisms) in a structure which has meaning and purpose. In terms of educational outcome, it should enable the individual to make a better contribution as a specialist by understanding his relationship with other specialists, and also to live a fuller life as a citizen outside his specialism. Breadth of curriculum of this kind is not achieved through multi-mini-specialism, even if some subjects are in contrasting subjects. It requires a genuine general component.

Within the broad foundation of the general element, the

most useful emphasis will be on human qualities that cannot be replaced by technologies, and on intellectual skills that involve value judgments and emphasise inter-personal skills. There will also be a need for appreciation of science and technologies, including information technologies, not only for specialists but for the majority of the population who will be affected by them.

Curriculum range 16–19

After the end of compulsory schooling, the whole of the three-element curriculum will not necessarily apply to all students. However, that does not imply that the whole is not appropriate for anyone or indeed for a majority.

The curriculum is delivered through the joint conscious activities of the staff of a college. Primarily, this will rest on the teaching staff, but all staff will contribute, particularly to the indirect curriculum. It is the responsibility of those who direct the non-teaching staff to ensure that everyone contributes to the indirect curriculum through the operation, influence and example of a style of community which promotes and respects the shared values indicated in the aims of the college. For teaching staff, there needs to be a clear understanding that the curriculum extends beyond the content of examination syllabuses. Delivery of a general educational curriculum should balance personal development and intellectual/skill development. Within intellectual/skill development there should be a balance of general education and differentiated specialist skill/knowledge development. All of these facets of the curriculum have an appropriate place at all stages in the growing maturity of the individual student. They must, therefore, be concurrent in the delivery of the curriculum, not consecutive. In other words, no aspect of the curriculum should be regarded as completed at a given age. The idea that the general comes earlier than the vocational or the specialist and can be ignored after a certain age is wrong. The relative balance may change from year to year as a student develops, but there is always potential for further development and maturity in both personal and general education.

It is unfortunate that current trends in curriculum development in non-advanced further education seems to be
in the direction of a consecutive curriculum. The major
further education examination bodies appear to have
adopted the assumption that the curriculum should progressively narrow the vocational focus. The worst manifestation
of this tendency is to think that the curriculum to age 14 +
should be general, that the curriculum from 14 + to 16 +
should be pre-vocational and that the curriculum after 16 +
should be specifically vocational.

Delivery of the curriculum

A college needs an explicit 'statement of aims'. Given such a
statement, it is possible to define a set of curriculum
objectives which will be the means of implementing the
'aims'. Curriculum objectives should include statements
about both the direct and the indirect curriculum; they
should define both general and specialist objectives if both
are included or implied within the 'aims', and they should
include reference to whether a particular objective applies to
all students, and if not, should state which group or groups
of students it does apply to. Some objectives will be pursued
via external qualifications. If the stated objectives of the
external qualification are the only ones relevant to the
students, then a description of objectives of that course may
be sufficient. If, however, other college aims or objectives
are to be pursued through the medium of that qualification,
then this must be made clear.

The process for curriculum delivery should start with the
writing, agreeing and publishing of a 'general statement of
aims', which should include an explicit statement of overall
curriculum intention and a definition of the groups of
students to whom the whole or, the various parts, apply.
Having agreed the statement, it is then a question of
negotiation for the level of resourcing needed to implement
that curriculum, followed by selection, appointment and in-
service development of staff to carry out the implementation.

The major decision for an institution is the relative

importance to be attached to the three main elements of the curriculum:

1. Education for personal development.
2. General intellectual/skill development.
3. Specialist intellectual/skill development.

Once the relative weighting in the curriculum for each group of students has been determined, time and energy must be allocated accordingly. An institution which places high priority on personal development and general education as compulsory elements for all, must allocate sufficient resources for effective delivery. It must also accept that it will be assessed, and its curricular effectiveness in these areas will be evaluated, as a prerequisite for continued resourcing.

This does not at first sound very different from what most people would recognise as the theory of current practice. All too often, especially in recent years, actual practice has had more to do with cutting whatever kind of curriculum coat could be got from an ever-decreasing piece of resourcing cloth, irrespective of whether the resulting coat covered what had originally been intended, let alone whether it was a good fit. All too often, the effective and general curriculum has been reduced and reduced, not by deliberate decision or by carefully ordered priorities but by force of circumstance and on the priority of least resistance.

Delivery of the curriculum – implications for the variety of institutional style

In a given geographical area, there will be students who will gain by the full three-element curriculum. Some will demand it, others will accept it if encouraged and persuaded by their surroundings. Others, however, may express a strong wish to be involved in only a part of the full potential curriculum.

The most appropriate environment for delivery of a full educational curriculum may not be the same as that which is appropriate for a specially vocational curriculum. Within the three-element curriculum, delivery of the first two elements, namely education for personal development and general intellectual/skill development, and especially the first, will depend a great deal on the style or ethos of the establishment. It will be more likely to succeed in a relatively small, cohesive, homogenous community in which staff and students can identify with shared beliefs, aims and objectives. Experience is showing that it will be most effective if the style of the whole organisation is designed primarily for the 16–19 age group.

Delivery of the third element, especially if a wide range of vocational specialisms is to be offered, will require a large establishment with a lot of specialist accommodation and equipment. The local authority, in partnership with colleges, will need to determine if and how a variety of environments can be provided. This may be in different institutions, each with an appropriate institutional style and distinctive curriculum range. Or, a variety of curriculum demands may need to be met within a single college.

In the 1950s the situation appeared simple. The two traditions were still separate, with school sixth forms and local technical colleges providing different ranges of specialisms and different styles of delivery. General education, with the traditional associated emphasis on personal development, was provided in schools; vocational preparation belonged in the colleges.

In the 1960s the general further education college emerged and took on the new role of providing A level subjects on a cafeteria basis, but usually without the general education element or the consciously provided curriculum for personal development. it was sometimes argued that mere presence in a more mixed environment with adult students provided for developing maturity. The provision of sixth form type examination courses in the further education environment came to be called 'the alternative route'.

In the 1970s we saw the growth and remarkable success of colleges designed, either exclusively or dominantly, for the 16–19 age group. The sixth form colleges were derived from the schools tradition but exploited the advantage of a purpose-designed environment for the age group. They provided an expanded curriculum, which incorporated more vocational relevance but retained an explicit personal and general element. The all-embracing tertiary colleges combined this role with that of the further education college.

They deliberately set out to provide the advantages of a rich environment with a strong 'indirect' curriculum, not only for those following traditional academic courses but also for those following vocational courses. Towards the end of the 1970s, the two traditions were clearly coverging.

The 1980s have, so far, shown a marked reversal of the trend of convergence. The emphasis in the further education sector is increasingly on work-related provision, entrepreneurial marketing and income-earning courses. Some colleges, especially sixth form colleges, feel that the full range of aims and objectives which they have regarded as important would not be well served by this change of emphasis. Although a number of single college tertiary reorganisations, planned some years ago, are still to be implemented, it seems likely that in future, authorities planning to reorganise 16–19 provisions will look to separate colleges. In an urban area, there may be a sufficiently large population to have a variety of institutions, each providing an appropriate style for the delivery of this curriculum. For example, there may be one or more sixth form colleges alongside one or more traditional further education colleges. We know from experience that this system can work effectively. If the sixth form colleges are offering a curriculum for the whole ability range, then this system can operate as a truly comprehensive tertiary system without selection of students but with selection by students and their parents of an appropriate curriculum. In large conurbations, the further education colleges may themselves have specialisms.

In small towns serving scattered populations, a single college may be the best way to serve all needs. In this case and in the current climate, increasing care will be needed to protect the right kind of environment for the full three-element full-time, general curriculum for 16–19s. There are certainly indications that current national policy will make the single tertiary college solution increasingly difficult, at least within its original concept.

In some areas it may become difficult to maintain the two alternative routes. If this is so, then the original route with the more complete curriculum must not be neglected. A simple takeover of A level teaching by a traditional further education college does not produce a genuine tertiary college. Such a move would lead to a diminution of curriculum delivery, which would be a serious loss to the educational system in any area where it was allowed to happen.

Curriculum delivery

Implications for internal organisation

Every college needs an internal organisation and management structure. The ultimate purpose of the structure is to facilitate curriculum delivery. A broad curriculum, emphasising personal development, will need an organisation based on broad professional leadership rather than simple resource management. A specific training curriculum will be better served by a specific management structure.

The curriculum is delivered by the staff; therefore, the purpose of structure is to make staff activity coherent, effective, curriculum-focused and as efficient as possible. The structure therefore needs to:

- organise the indivudal contributions of staff to produce a coherent whole;
- identify areas of leadership and responsibility for delivery of the various parts of the curriculum;
- co-ordinate and balance the various elements of the curriculum;
- organise appropriate groups of staff, students and resources of space and equipment, to come together for appropriate periods of time to undertake various kinds of curricular activity;
- reflect and enable the appropriate balance of priorities between various parts of the curriculum.

Because effectiveness of delivery depends entirely on the professional effectiveness of staff, the structure should also enable long term professional satisfaction, development and career progression of staff.

The following are three major areas of activity to be served by a staff structure:

1. Academic curriculum leadership, both general and specialist.

2. Personal pastoral curriculum leadership.
3. Administration.

Whether the structure separates or integrates these functions is fundamental. Whichever approach is adopted, a structure which does not provide a balance between them will fail to deliver the full curriculum effectively.

The structure of any college will be constrained by a number of factors, including national salary structures, local implementation of salary structures and historical salary levels of individual staff. Rarely will a college have the opportunity to adopt, 'ab initio', an ideal structure which entirely reflects its curriculum priorities. Most have inherited a structure in which subject departments predominate. Some have superimposed a faculty structure, and many have a pastoral structure which is sometimes separate and sometimes overlaps. In practice, most individual members of staff combine a subject responsibility with a cross-college and/or a pastoral role. Within some further education colleges this has been formalised as the matrix system, either two dimensional to incorporate cross-college responsibility and a subject role, or three dimensional to include in addition the personal/pastoral role. It has the advantage of giving more formal status to non-subject activity, but in some forms carries a danger of over-complexity and rigidity.

Perhaps the most important challenges that face internal college structures are:

– the need to relate new curriculum initiatives with each other and with traditional subjects;
– the need to support new curriculum developments which do not fit into traditional subject department patterns (CPVE, TVEI, etc);
– the need to support curriculum coherence for combinations of subjects which cross traditional groupings, such as sciences, humanities, etc;
– the need to provide refreshment, renewal and continuing professional satisfaction in a stable staff.

A possible model for an innovative structure would start by defining a number of areas of responsibility. These would then be identified with levels within the salary structure, either singly or in combination. Staff would be appointed to a level of seniority but not to a particular responsibility, and the structure would include a mechanism for movement of individuals between defined responsibilities from time to time. The list of responsibilities could change to meet changing circumstances. Individual staff could operate at a variety of levels according to topic, and lines of responsibility could be more complex than a simple pyramidal hierarchy, thus providing much wider opportunity for authority and leadership. Such a structure must, however, retain the key principle that the point of decision must coincide with the point at which 'the buck stops' for the element of the college's work.

Many sixth form colleges hoped that the recent change in teacher salary structures would have given them an opportunity to introduce new internal structures, reflecting a modern curriculum balance. The nature of imposed structure, with its automatic assimilation and aura of dispute and distrust, has not encouraged such restructuring. There are two important tests for any internal college structure. Firstly, does it facilitate or hinder delivery of the whole of the college curriculum? Secondly, does it support or hinder the right balance between various curriculum elements? If the answer to either of these questions is 'no', then the college must decide what freedom of manoeuvre, if any, it has for changes that will enable it to deliver the curriculum more effectively.

Implications for teaching style and staffing levels

Teaching style within an institution should be geared to the whole of the agreed curriculum. Clearly, for much of the working week style will be closely related to a particular section of subject content, but whatever content is being dealt with at a particular moment, the style of the teaching can and should serve the wider objectives of personal and general educational development if this is included in the overall curriculum for those students.

Having settled the objectives for groups of students, some degree of agreement will be needed between staff responsible for the delivery of the various parts of the curriculum. A combined and coherent staff strategy is needed, especially if the indirect element of the curriculum is regarded as important. If, on the other hand, objectives are limited to specialist skills and subjects, then the staff role can be nearer to that of subject instructor.

The following are among the personal and general curriculum objectives which can be effectively pursued through the vehicle of any or all items of subject content:

- understanding of, and effectiveness in, personal relationships;
- transmission of curiosity and excitement;
- respect for truth;
- the pursuit of excellence rather than competence alone;
- development of comprehension skills;
- development of oral, written, quantitative and spatial communication;
- development in the understanding of value judgments and their appropriateness;
- development of respect for objectivity and scientific methodology, and recognition of when it is appropriate.

Any or all of these are legitimate objectives within a full educational curriculum, to be pursued through teaching style in the study of appropriate content.

If all of these objectives are to be included within the curriculum, then the means of delivery of this part of the curriculum lies in the understanding, acceptance and determination of the whole teaching staff of the institution. For some staff, acceptance and understanding of this wide curriculum will come in part from initial professional training, but for most, this will need to be supplemented by in-service development.

Some institutions will determine a more limited curriculum, either for the whole of their operation or for specific groups of students. Such a limited group of objectives might consist entirely of a grouping of academic subject matter, or a collection of vocational skills. What is important is that the teachers delivering the curriculum know, understand and accept what it is that they are being asked to deliver. Not only must the institution be aware of the breadth of its curriculum, but those responsible for resourcing must also know and accept the implications, especially for staffing levels. A curriculum limited to subject knowledge or specific skills may be deliverable in large lectures, by use of modern technology rather than teachers, or by distance learning. A curriculum which also includes personal development and the general element, whilst using these techniques for effective transmission of knowledge and content, must also place emphasis on personal contact and interaction in suitable group sizes. Staffing levels for such a curriculum should be calculated according to local circumstances. A curriculum which incorporates a serious general or core element will involve students in additional class contact time, and this will require additional levels of resourcing, especially staff, in comparison with a curriculum which is limited to specialist objectives.

Qualifications and examinations

The curriculum is the means of achieving the 'aims'. Inevitably, in the present world this must include preparing students for their career. That means providing students with the opportunity to gain externally recognised qualifications. External qualifications are a very powerful influence on the curriculum and can, for good or bad, be an extremely important instrument in delivery of the curriculum. External examination syllabuses will affect the specialist areas of the curriculum most obviously, but a consequence is that if similar recognition is not given to the general area of the curriculum it may lose relative recognition among students and parents and, more dangerously, among staff.

Relatively few qualifications include explicit recognition of achievement in the indirect curriculum, with the consequence that this part of the curriculum has often been under-emphasised. On the other hand, confidential references have always played a major role in progression to higher education, and the development of records of achievement may help to increase recognition of the importance of effective delivery of the indirect curriculum.

Vocational qualifications

The recently established National Council for Vocational Qualifications has been given the task of reorganising vocational qualifications, on the basis of defining a vocational qualification as:

> a statement of competence . . . needed to facilitate entry into, or progression in employment and/or further education and training, which incorporates assessment to specified standards of:
> - skills
> - relevant knowledge and understanding
> - the ability to use skills and apply knowledge and understanding to the performance of relevant work related activities.

NCVQ expects standards of competence to be employment-led, and high among the Council's objectives is to provide vocational qualifications which are based on employment-led standards of competence. The existing variety and diversity of vocational qualifications grew up when people went into a job on leaving full-time education, expecting to remain in that job for the wole of their working life. The single-job working life is no longer the dominant pattern, and it is likely to become even less so. For the individual, and ultimately for the country, flexibility and transferability are now most important. The jungle of free-standing, unrelated vocational qualifications is no longer adequate, and we do need an overall framework which defines formal and readily understood links and relationships between the various task-specific qualifications. This should include credit transfer. It should, ideally, lead towards broad-based initial training with a 'credit bank' of qualifications that could be used, as necessary, for rapid in-service training to facilitate mid-career changes of role. If NCVQ can achieve this, it is to be warmly welcomed.

However, two of the five concerns expressed in the Review of Vocational Qualifications may be difficult if not impossible to reconcile. Namely, 'the unhelpful divide between so-called academic and so-called vocational qualifications should be bridged' and 'vocational qualifications should relate more directly and clearly to competence required in work'.

Much that has been written about the proposed new system of National Vocational Qualifications would appear to strengthen fears that, by giving insufficient recognition or credit for general educational qualifications, the divide between so-called academic and so-called vocational qualifications might be widened.

NVCQ has a challenging task. It could move us forward in developing an education/training scheme that will enable us to make a far more adaptable and flexible response to changing employment needs. But, if the battling vested interests force a narrowing solution, we could be much worse off.

General qualifications

Although not identical with the general curriculum in traditional further education, the so called 'sixth form curriculum' is included within the curriculum pattern of tertiary colleges, and its formal examination component corresponds closely with much of the general curriculum in further education. It has been under debate for many years. There are at least two major strands to the debate. The first and most discussed is the question of 'broadening'. This has centred on the role of A levels, their possible replacement and the role of general studies, complementary studies/non examined studies. The second major strand in the debate concerns the extension of the range of qualifications, so that students with a much wider range of ability could profit from a full post-16 general education curriculum. Balance of curriculum for the traditional group of students and extension of the range of the post-compulsory general curriculum are the major strands in the debate, but there are other important issues, including:

1. Change of emphasis within existing structures, e.g. the growth of new A levels in subjects which might be more relevant to the needs of modern society, such as

electronic systems, computer studies, industrial studies, business in society etc.

2. Changes in content and emphasis within existing subjects, e.g. changes in modern foreign languages, moving away from classical literature towards modern business applications.
3. Application of new technologies to learning strategies.
4. Distance learning and the application of educational technology etc.
5. Implications of the introduction of GCSE, especially in terms of the assessment experience which students will have gained.
6. The influence of new government initiatives, both for the 16–19 age group and for the compulsory sector, e.g. TVEI, the National Curriculum.

Breadth through qualifications

Perhaps the area of greatest interest, because it will also affect other areas, is that of A level. The government has asked for a review of A levels, but has implied that it does not wish to see fundamental change. Various suggestions have been made, including the replacement of the three-subject structure by a five-subject structure. The assumption still appears to be that any replacement will remain standards-based rather than competence-based. In other words, the qualification will be concerned with how well a candidate can understand/perform/apply, rather than a simple yes/no competence test on a list of items. There appears to be an assumption that five mini-specialisms will produce breadth, but whether this is justified is highly questionable.

Advanced supplementary level of GCE, (A/S), has been introduced as an add-on alternative to the old system. Its original concept of allowing two A levels and two A/S levels to replace three A levels, was intended to provide the possibility of increased breadth but it does not guarantee it. The concept has been extended by including the idea of complementary subjects which might be thought of as mini-specialisms, but also of contrasting subjects from different areas. Certainly, a curriculum offering a good range of both complementary and contrasting A/S levels available for free combinations with A levels, would allow significant numbers of bright youngsters to follow interesting and useful combinations. They would also allow more students to take newer subjects such as design, computer studies, information technology, etc. without feeling that they are over-committing themselves.

The International Baccalaureate has been operating for some years now, as an alternative to A levels. It is used in some independent international schools but is available to any school or college. It prescribes balance, and a 'theory of knowledge' course is compulsory for matriculation. Many people feel that it is suitable for the very top of the academic ability range but is not suitable for the range of students currently taking A levels.

Several unsuccessful attempts have been made to replace the A level system. The most recent, the N and F level proposals, failed after detailed and prolonged debate. Ironically, in spite of the fact that this proposal was intended to broaden the curriculum, much of the opposition to it was based on the fear that a five-specialist subject system would destroy the genuine breadth of general studies programmes currently offered in the best schools and colleges.

Perhaps the time was not then right for a root and branch replacement of A level; perhaps the rash of new developments, such as GCSE, TVEI, YTS, NCVQ etc., mean that the time will soon be right, but on balance this seems unlikely. A more promising way forward would be an evolutionary one.

An ideal examination structure for delivering a full educational curriculum would be one which offered a variety of levels, which could be combined in a variety of ways to suit a range of needs, but which for traditional students included the following:

1. Specialist study to the depth of existing A levels, but normally restricted to two subjects.
2. One or two specialist half A level subjects, at least one of which must be in a contrasting subject.
3. A general studies element, normally equivalent in time

allocation to an A level but designed as the unifying cement to set specialisms in context.

Such a structure would provide choice, allowing elements to be taken independently, but would also allow for rules of combination to be superimposed, similar to those of the International Baccalaureate, for example, to meet matriculation requirements for higher education. Elements could also be taken in combination with Mature GCSE or within prevocational courses.

Such an evolutionary change could be brought about by: progressive modification of A level syllabuses; development of A/S levels, especially in contrasting mode; giving greater emphasis and recognition to good general studies programmes in entrance requirements for Higher Education; and the introduction of guidelines or rules about combinations for matriculation.

Post compulsory, full-time general education is too important to risk the destructive effects of a disputed attempt at root and branch change. Change is needed, but an evolutionary approach would be not only safer but also more likely to succeed.

Range of general qualifications

The need for an extended range of general educational qualifications arises from the recognition that there is a need for a very much large proportion of the population to remain in full-time post-compulsory general education, laying an extended foundation for flexibility and the ability to train and retrain for a variety of tasks within a working career. This means that there is a need for a much wider spectrum of qualifications to cover a wider range of previous achievement, a wider range of ability and a wider range of career aspirations. This range will certainly include the opportunity to take the level of GCSE equivalent qualifications further, preferably without the well recognised problems that surrounded O level repeats.

The special needs of post-compulsory students for GCSE courses and qualification has been recognised in the GCSE (mature) qualifications. Unfortunately, many boards have, so far, given insufficient time to developing special GCSE(M) courses. problems are being experienced in delivering standard GCSE courses within one academic year, not in reaching standards, but in meeting coursework demands designed for two years. In any case, the demoralising effect on students – feeling that they are simply being offered a repeat of what they have done before – is bad. There is, therefore, urgent need to develop more mature GCSEs for 17 and 18 year-olds.

The range of general qualifications should also include courses of vocationally relevant general education, not orientated to any specific work-place or task, but which continue to develop general skills, especially those relevant to employment in general. Such courses should strengthen career prospects, whilst keeping options open by providing a basis for later career choice and specific training. The certificate of Pre-Vocational Education was originally intended to fulfil this need, but pressure to move in a more specifically vocational direction has been intense. There is now considerable doubt over whether it is anything like the whole answer, although many believe that its original curriculum concept remains valid.

The future

Many people have hoped for, and worked for, a convergence of the two major traditions. This has included a convergence of the curriculum. However, many now sense an end to that convergence. What, therefore, lies ahead?

The major post-16 change is the move towards market forces in the further education tradition. Employers are to have a much greater say in the control of the content, emphasis and delivery of the curriculum – certainly in the realm of NAFE. The Responsive College Programme, funded by the Manpower Services Commission now renamed as the Training Commission, gives employers the chance to tell further education chiefs what industry and commerce expect from colleges. This will be a test of how far employers are prepared to help reshape college objectives and programmes.

Inevitably, such employer-led market forces must be predominantly short-term.

The same trend is clear in the work of the National Council for Vocational Qualifications. The Council recognises the need for general skills, such as communication, knowledge and understanding. However, general education seems to be relegated to a secondary, 'underpinning' role relative to work-place relevant competences. Indeed, it is becoming clear that in the new NCVQ, considerations of personal development and general education will take a low priority in comparison with immediate employment needs. This reflects government thinking, in that the terms of reference given to the NCVQ clearly stated the priority of work-place competence. This trend must inevitably, and perhaps rightly, determine the curriculum priority for not only NAFE but for all vocational qualifications.

The position, standing and provision of general education is becoming more difficult, especially in colleges which are basically further education institutions. For some students in work-related NAFE, these new developments will lead to a more effective curriculum. They may also lead to a more effective delivery of that type of curriculum. Many students, and arguably an increasing proportion of the age group, should, however, be following a broad-based personal curriculum. Their needs must be met, including those that are served by an environment with broader objectives than work-relatedness.

For sixth form colleges within the schools system this may be relatively straight forward. Developments in qualifications, such as GCSE Mature, A/S levels and revision of A levels, will be watched with care and implemented as appropriate. Local financial management may or may not help to strengthen the delivery of the personal curriculum. New conditions of service for staff may make it desirable for the published curriculum to be more explicit, ensuring that non-timetabled activities are recognised as a part of each teacher's professional task of contributing to the delivery of the whole curriculum. Colleges will watch with care the attitude of government to the maintained sector. Most have excellent relationships with the LEA and wish to maintain them, but if, as some fear, the maintained sector above age

14 + is to be turned over to the work-related tradition, with broad education being left to the independent sector, then a number of colleges may wish to retain the option of grant maintained status, if they believe that this will provide the best support for effective delivery of the full personal curriculum.

For colleges combining the full personal curriculum for some students, with a work-related, non-advanced further education curriculum for others, the situation could be a good deal more complex and much may depend on the membership and priorities of new governing bodies. Will it be possible to convince the predominant employer representatives on governing bodies of tertiary colleges that such colleges need to meet the needs of full-time general education students, as well as those following work-related courses? It seems likely that established tertiary colleges with a firmly established role in relatively small towns have support and will maintain that role. Further education colleges with a smaller general education role may find it more difficult.

Conclusion

There are stirring and challenging times ahead for the post-16 curriculum and for those with the task of delivering it. Changes will be necessary, but not every proposed change will be for the good. In the midst of change we must strive to recognise what will be of long term value, and we must retain what we know is good. As the various band-waggons thunder by, we must watch closely and pick off the 'goodies'. We must ensure, however, that we don't get carried away and that we are not bowled over by the next one which is sure to be coming along close behind.

8 Staff development

Shaun McLoughlin

In the beginning – promotion and transfer

In 1979, Oswestry reorganised along comprehensive lines. The two single-sex grammar schools and four secondary modern schools became four 11–16 comprehensive, and the small college of further education became a tertiary college.

One of the difficulties with any reorganisation is the less than free hand that one has in trying to accommodate all the staff previously in the system. Inevitably, during the protracted redistribution phase, some will gain well-deserved promotion; some will not, however well deserved. A few will experience, for a variety of reasons, a real or apparent demotion. A very few, perhaps two or three per cent, will appeal. At the end of the exercise, it is inevitable that some staff are going to be disappointed. There is no way of totally avoiding this, although it is quite clear what an employer needs to do about it. The potentially damaging effects of disenchanted staff should not be ignored – yet they often are. This is where good, carefully thought-out manpower planning and management strategies must come into play, with the whole question of review and staff development being the vehicles.

Initial integration

There has always been a mutual mistrust between schools and further education sectors and a reluctance, even at Department of Education and Science level or at LEA level, to break down the barriers. A commonly held belief is that, in some way, the staff are just as different as the students and pupils. Yet one of the fascinating aspects of the early reorganisation period is that during the first term of operation, ex-further education staff and ex-schools staff discover that they are both engaged in a similar exercise and that they can actually talk the same language. Admittedly, some of the staff had a little initial difficulty in realising what a comprehensive range of student capability had to be catered for, but even that soon diminished.

Overall, it is very heartening indeed to see mutual mistrust give way to wary regard and, a little later, to mutual respect and support. The odd pocket of resistance occasionally manifests itself, but retirements and changes of staff over eight years have all but removed them altogether. One of the most heartening developments was when NATFHE and AMMA formally agreed to co-operate and act in unison within the college. This one act had far-reaching implications in terms of developing an accord between the unions and management.

The need for review

All staff need to be valued and feel valued – regularly. Employers and their managers need to work together to deliver an essentially simple review process. It is a pity that so many years have been wasted because of the rather insensitive introduction some years ago, by the then Secretary of State, of the idea of a potentially punitive staff appraisal system, with the inevitable union reaction. Had common sense prevailed, we could have had a simple review in operation three or four years ago, targetting a staff development policy.

If we adopted a simple basic strategy we might come up with a relatively straightforward approach which would not be threatening in any way to anyone but rather, very supportive.

Strategy

Where are we now?
Where do we need to go to?
What factors are preventing us?
What do we need to do to remove the hurdles?
What training is necessary to achieve our goals?

Approach (A college review)

Where is the college now?
Where does it need to go in the next five years?
What are the changing responses required regarding

- industrial needs
- MSC initiatives
- Government initiatives
- Technology implications
- Community needs

What is stopping the college responding?

- external factors
- internal factors

What needs to be done to remove any hurdles?

- short term
- medium and long term
- attitudes

What limitations should the college place on itself?

- what can it do?
- what could it do if it used the expertise available to it?
- what should it do?
- what should it not do?

Out of this analysis of the whole college needs (a college audit), conducted by at least the senior management team, there should emerge a college policy statement. It needs to make clear where it is going and what it can and cannot do. Then one can begin to review the sections within the college by similarly asking the following series of questions:

Where is the section now?
Where does it need to go? (Annual target setting within college policy.)
What prevents it from achieving its targets?

- external factors, both within and outside the college

- internal factors within section
- staff and expertise shortages, and attitudes in a generic sense.

What needs to be done to enable the section to go forward along the target pathway?
What are the training needs of the section?

This part of the analysis needs to be conducted by one or two senior managers, depending upon the functional structure of the management matrix.

This may consist of a head of department only, or a director of curriculum and a director of staff development policy, and it must include the section leader and all staff within the section. It is important therefore to deal with manageably small sections at a time.

The important point to stress is that no individual member of staff should, or needs, to feel threatened by what is effectively an overall review of targets, and training needs analysis at this stage of the process. It has not been a personal appraisal situation in any way; it is a college/section review process.

The final stage is the process which, if handled sensitively and professionally, will naturally follow on and lead towards an understanding of individual needs and aspirations. It is only at this point that individual review sessions should be orchestrated, but by this time everyone should have gained a far better perspective and understanding of what needs to be done. In most cases the need for personal development and inservice training will have been accepted. There are very few staff who are not aware of their own shortcomings or are unwilling to undertake structured training to help themselves gain in expertise and self-confidence.

The individual staff reviews need to be negotiated with whoever they elect, and should normally be a line manager, though it will very much depend on the circumstances. Whoever undertakes the review must give commitment to it and transmit the agreed outcome to the staff development co-ordinator, who can arrange whatever training may be decided upon. Clearly, it is imperative to regard the whole process as an enhancing one which will not only improve the college's responsiveness to changing demands but will improve the individual lecturers own expertise, self-confidence and respect. It should never, ever, be regarded as an appraisal process with an attendant punitive connotation. That would not only be counter-productive but positively damaging to the morale of a service at present under constant threat from so many, often conflicting and ill-thought-out, central initiatives at an ever increasing rate. The whole process is one of agreed negotiation on a professional level; not a personal one. At least, bearing in mind the one or two per cent who may not respond to this kind of process and who could become a disruptive influence, there is now a properly constituted disciplinary procedure for teaching staff, and for the sake of the 99 per cent managers and employers need to use it. There is nothing worse for staff than to see a colleague 'getting away with it'.

Career planning and in-service training

Most teachers at some time in their lives wish to progress in a career pattern, though a number of them, for a whole variety of reasons, some of which are beyond immediate control, e.g. family commitments, may 'stick' in one place. The good managers therefore need to turn their attention to the needs of at least two groups of staff; the upwardly mobile and what is often called the stable core. This latter group can all too often become a reactionary core which may positively impede the proper evolutionary development of the college. Conscious efforts need to be made to involve this group in developmental work to maintain both their interest and commitment. Properly handled they are the 'salt of the earth'.

The upwardly mobile

Generally speaking lecturers are well motivated, enthusiastic, innovative and sometimes entrepreneurial. The real 'go-getters' may have a new idea off the wall everyday and may need a careful filter system to restrain some of their wilder ideas, but care needs to be taken not to restrain them too far and quench the spark. Too little management and it will be like riding a bucking bronco, never being quite sure where it will take you. Too much and the high flier will either leave before he has had time to contribute very much, become frustrated, switch off, even become positively disruptive, or what is often worse, end up under severe stress and start to suffer from stress-related health problems. More stress may be generated through the delaying or avoidance of progressive decision-making than is ever caused by the occasional mistake of a positive decision-maker.

Delegation of responsibility with executive authority has an uplifting effect on staff, the college, and ultimately the clients. Above all, we need to encourage able colleagues to develop themselves and to give their expertise to the college while on their rightful way up the career ladder.

It is a curious fact that while we pay lip service to looking for and developing entrepreneurial approaches, we seem to have built a negative bureaucratic system to prevent this very activity. Consequently, what essentially has become the English, characteristically ambivalent, attitude towards the profit motive has developed. We espouse success but when faced with it we try to play it down. It is acceptable to have wealth but not quite so acceptable to wish to make it. It is an interesting psychological situation which has surely contributed to the apparent inability to respond as a strong nation in the now highly competitive world.

Risk-taking is anathema and yet is imperative for success. The English are peculiarly adept at finding a dozen reasons as to why one should not do something new, but they are singularly inept at finding one good reason why one should! It has become a national characteristic. Does it need to remain as such? Why do we resist change with such energy? We need the entrepreneurs, the risk-takers and all the progress that comes with them. We need to nurture those staff displaying these characteristics – not muzzle them.

The stable core

The good, solid, dependable and conscientious teachers form the backbone of any organisation. We all have them and we depend heavily upon them. How often do we take them for granted and even regard some of them as pedestrian, or even dull? We certainly often undervalue them, and yet by so doing we can indeed promote the switch-off or the deviant behaviour pattern, where the perceived incentive becomes how to obtain early retirement with suitable enhancement.

Why should we accept the current trend where staff who, for a variety of reasons, may be either underperforming, going off the rails of acceptability or have just switched off, are offered opportunities of early retirement, often with substantial enhancement, while the good, solid, hardworking, effective staff who may be getting tired have virtually no chance of obtaining such opportunities. There have been too many generous golden handshakes given to the trouble-maker or incompetent in recent years. Isn't it time we rewarded our successes and not our failures? They deserve our support, encouragement and rewards.

For this group, personal development in career terms may not be a priority, though all will need some updating in specific skill areas to cope with change. What they do require is encouragement towards increased self-confidence. They need to be valued. They may need help with personal or professional problems. They do not deserve to be ignored.

Indeed, much of their self-development may take place within the college rather than on specific in-service training courses. This is where the prudent managers will try and organise their time so that they can walk the job, make themselves available when staff want to see them, be sensitive and sympathetic to peoples needs, be good listeners and encourage and congratulate success.

Throughout it is very important to develop mutual trust within teams of people, delegate responsibility and authority as widely as possible to enable people to perform effectively and review needs and progress. In these ways the manager is striving to capitalise on strengths and help weaknesses, treating the whole business as one of managing in a positive way.

In-service training control

Out of all this a coherent staff development programme for all staff needs to be formulated, not forgetting that clerks and technicians require in service training and development just as much as teaching staff.

TRIST, over the last year or two with all its eleventh hour ad-hoccery and retrospective planning, was not as helpful as it might have been. Severe disruption of learning sessions was in grave danger of negating the very improvements it was trying to engender. When GRIST first arrived on the scene, it appeared to go the other way and demanded that everything should be planned up to 15 months in advance. But as it settles down it would appear to be giving us a chance to forward plan quite a lot of training, at the same time giving us a degree of flexibility. It means we now have a mechanism for generating the coherency of training, which, in conjunction with the WRNAFE forward planning, is leading us towards a proper 'business planning' position. Increased professionalism should result in an increased ability to respond to real needs, not the marketing myopia or wheelbarrow marketing that has bedevilled further education for so long. It is interesting to note that when researching one college's training needs for the 1988–89 GRIST bid, there were no less than 24 areas of training required, ranging from GCSE and TVEI to Open Learning and Modular Based Course Operation, and from management skills for section leaders and IT for all managers to financial control and evaluation. The need for training is as great as it has ever been and has to be very directly attributable to the revolution we are experiencing, with every new development requiring implementation by the day after publication.

Ever changing change

TVEI, GCSE, A/S levels, CPVE, YOP and subsequent YTS schemes, ATS, JTS, Community Programmes and their latest amalgamation, and of course, the National Curriculum implications, along with local financial management, net-budgeting and local industry training needs, have all arrived on the educational scene within the last few years, at an ever increasing pace. Perhaps one could be forgiven for wondering how these often conflicting needs can be amalgamated into a coherent, all-embracing curriculum package, and how the training needs of staff might be organised to fulfil the implicit obligations. One might also be forgiven for hoping that someone will be able to help the chalk-face lecturer to cope with it all. But who is it to be?

Sadly, it becomes clearer every day that whenever conflicting needs or potential confusing situations are pointed out to the policy makers, and advice is sought, there develops the 'glazed look' response. Politicians say 'Oh that is for the local authorities to solve' or 'the schools and colleges will have that delegated down to them'. There appears to be an amazing naivety that hard-pressed staff can spend their time solving often very difficult problems and implement policy decisions, often with scant guidelines. There is a demonstrable need here for direct interpretational help to be given and suitable digested guidelines to be issued – perhaps a role for the advisory service? The GCSE is a case in point – the sheer workload created by confused and contradictive guidelines for staff, with the current fifth years as the guinea pigs, is going to create a problem or two for a college's 16 + intake for September 1988. What will staff be required to do about it? No November resits will be available – does that mean that more students will have to accept a three-year programme? Is that going to be a disadvantage or an advantage to them?

The now classic case of MSC, not only reorganising itself practically every month, changing the goal posts nearly every week, and indeed, at times, nearly every day, has led to the situation where many within MSC are now saying that if they don't experience a major change at least every 10 days they start to suffer from withdrawal symptoms!

How can those at institutional level cope with the apparent contradictions between the National Curriculum's single-subject pigeon-holed approach [of circa] 1905 and the cross-curricular understanding and interplay we have sought through TVEI, CPVE, the Schools Curriculum Development Committee's national campaign in the arts entitlement area and others? And yet, that is precisely what they are expected to do – not by design but, once again, by default. No one else will do it, and so increasingly it becomes clear that the job of the principal and that of senior management at large will be to filter all these ideas and initiatives, digest them as decently as possible and try to blend them into a coherent pattern for delivery by the staff. Is this what the job should be in a well directed, more centralist system?

The whole picture is changing so rapidly that there is difficulty in keeping up with it, which is bad enough, but what about the clients? Once the packages are put together they have to be sold to potential clients, young and not so young, to parents whose perceptions of education may go back a fair way and to industry who, even now, have not really fully understood CSE. It is perhaps not so surprising that many people are hankering after A levels again, however inappropriate they may be. It is at least a readily understood qualification which has been around for a long time.

Clearly, it is of extreme importance that all clients are helped to a clearer understanding of what is a very confusing and confused plethora of qualifications. This means more need in terms of in-service training for staff; marketing a corporate college image and coherent curricula packages is a skill only just emerging.

Accepting that over the next few years the stable situation will be instability, it is interesting to note how we reacted when Information Technology burst on the scene. Every school was encouraged to obtain a computer so that all would be solved! It is only now, several years later that the full realisation of the implications is dawning. Only now is the necessary software becoming available to drive the machines, and we are beginning to train operators to use the programs. We are still very short of highly trained technicians who can help the users, not only to exploit the systems available, but to troubleshoot when the machinery 'goes down'. Without this fully trained backup and teachers who are trained to exploit the potential, whether it is in mathematics, history, technology, design or management for example, the humble computer becomes mere junk.

How many firms have been sold a computer which did not answer their needs? How little money was invested in training? How often have we been expected to take all this on board 'within our existing resources'? And yet, how much venture capital is really needed if we are to make the most of the marvellous potential offered to us in our management information systems? We appear reluctant to invest in the future and to learn by our mistakes. Updating skills have never been so important. Never have we apparently spent so much money on it, and yet, it is still often too little, too late and in yesterday's direction instead of tomorrow's.

This does not mean that every senior manager should also become an accomplished computer operator; even worse, a computer programmer. The proposal is to train enough computer operators, technicians, programmers and, above all, what used to be called systems analysts, to help a principal to adapt the ways in which, he or she, as a manager, needs to operate and to exploit the IT potential. To reconcile objectives in a compatible way with the sheer potential that a good, well-conceived MIS system can give would enable a principal to be far better informed, and thus a more effective manager than would ever be possible using only manual methods. Computers do not save money – a commonly held misconception. It is not sensible to try and put a traditional or even outmoded control system into computers. Technology makes one think differently and develop new ways of managing, and so it should. All this requires training, and a lot of it.

Gone are the days when principals were seen as the educational leader, concerned only with the curriculum; the job, increasingly, is to manage a complex system and to become a highly proficient, entrepreneurial financial controller, none of which many have been trained for. It is often surprising though how little help can be found from within the service to enable senior staff to cope with these changes. There is constant disappointment in the attempts of educationalists to run management seminars, some of which have little to say in terms of crisp management techniques, and some of which are so weighted down by erudite academicism as to be practically useless. The financial control systems practised by LEAs can often be more of a hindrance to good financial control than a help, and are almost always historical in their concept. Under net budgeting, there is a need to know from day to day exactly where a principal is and for him to be able to predict ahead.

Never before has there been such a need to develop an expertise through the formation of 'partnership contracts'.

The LEA, college, industry, careers and other services all need to input into the overall strategy. With well thought out partnership strategies success can be achieved.

The academic board

As a management tool, the academic board is unfortunately vulnerable to misuse or even abuse. Cases of NATFHE taking over and holding the management to ransom have occurred. At the other end of the spectrum, management have almost ignored it, and indeed in some colleges it may not even meet, other than spasmodically. And yet, it can be, and should be, and in many colleges is, a valued method of managing. Though sixth form colleges do not have mandatory articles of government in quite the same way as tertiary colleges do, there is much merit in both kinds of college using the board as a vehicle for detailed involvement of staff at all levels in decision-making processes, at least in specified areas.

Under the terms of the articles of government, the governors are charged with arranging the formation of the academic board, whose members include the principal (ex officio chairman), the vice principal, heads of department and at least six elected members of staff. It is in choosing the latter that care must be exercised. It is important to have all sections of a college represented, for example by stipulating at least one member of staff from each faculty, division or department, the chief administrative officer, the college librarian, the co-ordinator of community education and one or two student representatives. In addition, the local careers officer can be co-opted.

The mandate of the academic board, again according to the articles of government, may vary from LEA to LEA but is principally that of an advisory body and not an executive one. Its actions are subject to the principal's and to the governors approval.

The board's principal areas of concern are the entry and examination of students, the whole area of curriculum provision and delivery, including concern over developing areas, and changing needs. Increasingly, it needs to respond to market research and it is directly involved in agreeing the final pattern of work-related, non-advanced further eduation to be submitted via the WRNAFE plan to MSC. It also needs to turn its attention towards predicting changes to cope with a clear need for forward planning, while at the same time coping with the apparent restrospective planning of central government guidelines.

If anything, the Academic Board can be increasingly useful, not only as a planning tool but as a monitoring device, since it will often pick up small details needing attention which would otherwise be easily overlooked. Since it is open to outsiders, both as members and as witnesses, the level of activity is both professional and productive and can help individuals enormously in their own professional development, through not only realising the perspectives of an across college overview, but by taking an active part in formulating college policy and direction.

The unions

It is difficult to talk about union involvement and its effects upon staff development other than from personal experience, but certainly from some of the reported actions one sadly gains the impression, all too often, of conflict. In the end, conflict leads to a no-win situation. Everyone loses out; staff, management, government, and not least, and always damagingly, students.

Sadly, so much of the conflict has been exacerbated by clashes of political ideologies and, certainly, by a great deal of pigheadedness on the part of employers and union, with very little help and practically no integrity being displayed by government. The sooner there is recognition that all sides have some basic professional rights, duties and dignity, perhaps there can be a return to a professionally conducted, planned debate on what education should be about and what investment should be made in the education and training process.

Amidst all the debilitating action and growing despondency, with consequent lowering of morale over the last few years (not helped at all by the now quite unacceptable differentials between schools and further education salaries, particularly at senior management levels), somehow accord has to be maintained. It is vitally important, in a period of unprecedented and accelerating rates of change, that all interested parties – government, employers, unions, educationists and related services – stop trying to short change each other and recognise that, without massive investment in effective training for the future, this country will fail to achieve success.

We need to be able to plan, under GRIST, ESG, ESF and the host of other planned initiatives, a coherent staff development programme with confidence that it will not be disrupted by all kinds of interventionist activity. At local level we can achieve that, and indeed in many colleges there has always been an excellent working relationship with the two main unions, NATFHE and AMMA. Partnerships do not happen by accident; they have to be worked at very hard. But over the question of staff review and development there is no doubt at all that without the political manoeuverings at national level and consequent embargo by the union on anything to do with appraisal, that left to their own devices, there would have been a proper review process in many colleges some three years ago. The structure of staff development could have been so much better co-ordinated than it is at present, and without doubt would have led to much increased self-confidence and higher levels of expertise in staff, with enviable increases in standards of teaching.

Special needs

When the 1981 Education Act was enacted, it was thought that there would be much more commitment towards making provision for the spectrum of special needs in the 16–19+ age range than there had been. It is only now, six years later, that any real commitment has emerged, and even then it is patchy.

In 1981, in one college, it was considered whether they should go into this field. Thought was given to what obligations should be developed, what the implications were going to be for all and what limits should be set. The support from all staff was overwhelming. The eventual response from all the agencies involved in any way with handicap was magnificent, and today there is a superb learning support unit, the largest adult basic education programme in the area using over 150 volunteers and paid staff.

Staff across the college are involved, since the view is taken that, as far as possible, these students will be positively integrated into mainstream courses.

Over the last two years the staff have been shown how to cope with the handicapped in a more structured way than before. There are perhaps several schools of thought as to how one goes about it. Demonstrations and presentations are often made on specific aspects which undoubtedly help, but so often the requirements of the individual student are so unique that rather than try and turn everyone into a special needs specialist, it is a question of helping each member of staff with the individual case as far as possible. Two care assistants help enormously, and it means there is always someone whom staff can call on. This way of helping staff is rather more effective than large inputs of INSET in special needs training. But it is an area which is woefully inadequately funded. After all, a 12:1 staff-student ratio, as with mainstream work, is not exactly relevant or feasible with this kind of work.

Broadly, there are five levels of staff training, four of them being aimed at all staff who come into contact with special needs young people. They are delivered by the small learning support team, who:

1. Provide a general level of awareness and preparation, via acticles in the staff newsletter or informal chats.
2. Give individual support to staff, 30 to 40 in the college, who are trying to integrate, mainly physically handicapped, students into mainstream courses. Help with specific health problems affecting learning, or with specific backup remedial skills and expertise.
3. Have developed many links with staff from YTS schemes, ATCs care staff and others. These staff, more often than not, are not trained teachers and need help in coping with the less able young people. This help may be through INSET courses organised by learning

support staff or it may be through workshops run by outside bodies, such as the National Bureau of Handicapped Students. The CGLI Teaching of Special Needs in Further Education course, which is relevant for some who wish to perhaps develop a much greater understanding, is also available.

4. Help teaching staff who find themselves teaching people with special needs for a large proportion of their time, particularly those of whom are part-time, though qualified teachers, and who need a great deal of information on the young people's problems on an individual basis, help with background resources; medical, learning and above all supportive counselling.

5. Continually update the special needs tutors themselves so that they can remain informed.

16 + planning

In many areas there are now moves to co-ordinate 16 + planning across the spectrum of provision, involving the 11–18 schools and the variety of post-16 colleges. This should lead to the development of a coherent policy for the education and training of those who volunteer to continue after their period of statutory schooling, as well for those who, as adults, return on a part-time basis. This should create opportunities for the staff from both schools and colleges to work and train together in a more meaningful way than at present. This may well help to eliminate, at least to some extent, the mutual mistrust which, sadly, still exists between teachers in the two sectors. This will be to the benefit of those for whom the whole educational system exists – the students.

9 Postscript

Simon Lambert

The preceding sections have illustrated some of the particular needs and necessities for the establishment and running of post-16 colleges. There has to be a clear will on the part of the local education authority to press on with their agreed proposals, despite the apparent difficulties which the existing legislation appears to put in their way. This determination has to be based on majority public support, or, at the very least, a minority opposition obtained through a wide-ranging and open consultative procedure. This procedure, if it is to be successful, has to establish a foundation of public information about the existing system and its strengths and its weaknesses, an understanding of the possible solutions to the stated problems and the reasoning which has led to the formulation of the proposed plans for change. Having obtained the approval of the Secretary of State for the implementation of the proposals and the development of the new colleges, it is essential to maintain the confidence and morale of the staff in the existing institutions and to establish an air of optimism amongst those will be involved in the building up of the new system. The emphasis on the newness of the colleges must be paramount; the fact that they will be managed in new ways, that the staffing structure will be changed and reinforced, that the ability range of the potential students will be wider and that, above all, they will not simply be the old institutions, or parts of them, under new names, must be given prominence. This last point underlines, again, the need for different management structures when new types of colleges are opened. The concept of the traditional FE department – autonomous and sometimes almost isolated – needs to be modified but not necessarily totally abolished. There must, however, be a centralisation of certain major functions to guarantee that there will be a liberal and unbiased recruitment policy, an equitable distribution of resources and a college-based curriculum rather than a series of discrete departmental initiatives. If such changes were to be accepted throughout the whole further education system, and not just in the tertiary colleges, then the image and the nature of the system would change and the colleges would be seen as more responsive to the real, as opposed to the assumed, needs of students and less concerned with their apparent internal competiveness. In the sixth form colleges, which have inherited the very different school-type departmental structures, there are fewer pressures on students to choose subjects other than those that are most suitable for their needs. Courses can be more diverse, and the determining factors are the demands of higher education and, to a much lesser extent, an occasional rigidity in the college timetable. This latter problem is becoming less constraining as colleges increase in size, giving a far greater flexibility than was ever possible in school sixth forms. The emphasis should be clearly upon the identification of the needs of the potential students. These needs, however loosely stated by the young people themselves, have to be translated and facilitated into a coherent set of demands by the specialised staff and agencies of careers teachers and careers officers. Pre-course requirements, i.e. GCE or GCSE subjects and grades, cannot be ignored – they introduce an element of realism into the choice of course. Satisfaction and success are the key stones of a tertiary system.

Since the beginning of the present decade there appears to have been a greater acceptance by parents, in particular, of the necessity for some form of post-16 reorganisation. The impact of falling rolls, the educational disadvantages of small sixth forms, the widening of the curriculum, the demands for more and better vocational and pre-vocational training and the undoubted success of the new colleges, sixth form and tertiary, have all contributed to this new climate of opinion. Of course, there is still opposition when an LEA proposes change; nostalgia for the sixth form, unfounded suspicion of further education and political influence and bias all play their part. In recent years the DES has been more constructive, though dogmatism is still evident and some wide-ranging schemes of tertiary reorganisation, such as the one in Sheffield, have been subject to the same erosion as was evident in Manchester prior to their 1982 16–19 system. Nevertheless, in the 1980s more colleges were opening and a number of the existing sixth form colleges were being transformed into tertiary colleges.

In those areas where opposition to 16+ change is still evident, the basis for this reaction is still the same as it was when the early colleges were being planned. From the schools the almost automatic responses are:

1. An expressed desire to keep their sixth forms, however small, uneconomic and educationally unsatisfactory they are.

2. The claim that the loss of the sixth form would lead, because of the Burnham points system where resources are allocated on a pupil numbers/age basis, to a financial penalty expressed through staff, books, equipment and ancillary help.

3. The belief that teachers enjoy, and feel that they are entitled to, sixth form teaching, and a school which cannot offer this level of teaching would be at a disadvantage compared with those that can.

4. The claim that schools can offer a system of care and guidance for their 16+ pupils which, because of the time that these pupils have already spent in the school, cannot be matched in a two-year period in a college.

5. That sixth form pupils have the opportunity to exercise a degree of leadership over the younger pupils and that both groups benefit from this.

These arguments and statements have changed very little over the years, and, given the access to parents enjoyed by the heads of schools, they are often accepted without demur. They are, however (except the first which is emotional not practical), demonstrably false, and in areas with either sixth form or tertiary colleges they can be seen to be false. The resources argument can, in any case, be countered by LEA policy. However, the mythology, like all mythology, persists and the proposed legislation recently published by the Secretary of State may give parents the opportunity of putting their beliefs into practice. If an LEA is proposing a reorganisation, which would lead to their secondary schools being restricted to an 11–16 age range, thus losing their sixth forms, then the governors of these schools, who will be parent-dominated in any case, can arrange a ballot of all the parents on whether to apply to the Secretary of State to allow the school to opt out of the control of the LEA and to be funded directly from the DES on a grant-maintained basis. Even if the governors do not wish to initiate such a ballot, if a sufficient number of parents are so inclined then they can demand that the governors organise such a poll. Given this possibility, it may be that an LEA will be discouraged from making tertiary proposals. However, a little thought might suggest that the continued existence of a school, or schools, with sixth forms alongside post-16 colleges is not unusual. This situation already exists in the areas where the voluntary aided schools retained their sixth forms when the county schools became 11–16. It is also salutary to remember that it is the parents who are voting, not the potential students, and that these students may well wish to attend an institution which is specifically designed to satisfy their needs, and not one which must be organised with the work and attendance of younger children in mind. They may well decide to leave school and attend the college; this phenomenon is evident in areas which already have a mixture of sixth forms and colleges.

It is to be hoped that the strength of an LEA's commitment to the fulfilment of the ideals of greater participation, wider choice of course and parity of esteem, that are so evident in the existing tertiary systems, will bolster their confidence to proceed with their plans despite the threatening noises from some groups of parents.

There are, however, other factors which are influencing the concepts of a tertiary system. The introduction of TVEI in 1982, funded not through the DES but through the MSC, with its emphasis on 14–18 continuity, can be a two-edged sword for the colleges. It encourages an emphasis on partnership between those institutions providing pre-16 education and those others offering post-16 education and training. This partnership, as a reading of an earlier section will show, is an essential and successful part of the work and organisation of the colleges. Beginning as the response to an obvious need for pastoral continuity, it now encompasses a whole range of curricular initiatives – a true partnership in fact, as well as theory. The impact of the TVEI schemes could, should, and does, in some of the areas which adopted the project in its early stages, reinforce the idea of partnership. However, the concept of a 14–18 continuum could give strength to the arguments in favour of the retention of sixth forms; the apparent advantages of continuity in the same institution with same staff and the difficulties of examination board compatibility being only two of these.

The drive by the DES to establish a new type of school in urban areas, the City Technology College, could also affect the establishment, and, to a lesser extent, the existence of a 16+ college. It is clear that this new breed of school, 11–18, sponsored and, thus, influenced by commerce and industry, will, even if they do not inherit the traditional school sixth form image, attract able students. This factor will modify the range of ability of those students who choose to enrol in a college. Although not set up directly in competition with the colleges, one hopes, but as a mechanism designed to improve the present school system and to introduce a greater degree of industrial and commercial awareness amongst their pupils, they will, without doubt, introduce an element of competitiveness for students wherever they are established.

The setting up of the well-funded (and to a large extent independent of the DES) National Council for Vocational Qualifications provides yet another cause for concern over the future of the tertiary sector. A comparision of the plans for a national curriculum, proposed in the new legislation, with its periodic assessments of pupils on a subject basis, with the NCVQ proposals for vocational relevance and competence and its system of modular assessment, surely reinforces the old 'academic/vocational' divide. This divide was disinterred, after a period of partial burial, by the 1984 White Paper 'Training for Jobs', which led to the LEAs having to present their plans for work-related, non-advanced further education to the MSC who now control a significant amount of the funding. So there is, yet again, a division of responsibility, and the situation is even more confused by the proposal in the new Education Bill for LEA plans for further education to be submitted to the DES.

So, what of the future? The existing sixth form colleges are unlikely to suffer from the changes proposed and implemented in further education, brought about either by the MSC or NCVQ. In fact, they may gain students who, though having ambitions which could be best met through the vocational route, are disinclined to relinquish their academic interests to do so. The increase in the pre-vocational work in the sixth form colleges and their close involvement with the schools in areas where TVEI schemes have been introduced are in their favour. They are as likely to be affected by the reduction in the size of the 16–19 age group as any other set of institutions, but they have a well-established record of improving the post-16 participation rate wherever they have been established, and so they should survive. There may even be colleges where the parents of the students vote to take the college out of the control of the LEA but this seems unlikely. The establishment of the new colleges will, of course, be subject to this peril when parents are persuaded to try and 'protect their school', but perhaps common sense and study of the success of the existing colleges will prevail.

For the tertiary colleges the picture does appear more gloomy. Given the competition for students, from which they have, up to now, been protected but which could develop from 'opted-out' schools with sixth forms and from the City Technology Colleges, they may well become much less comprehensive in their intake and thus their character could change. The smaller the college the more likely this is to happen. The pressures to conform to central government planning for vocational training will be great; funding will become more specific, the power of the vocational department could be re-established, idealism will suffer and retrenchment will be the order of the day.

The quest for more students taking more vocational courses may have led those who plan the overall provision for the 16–19 age group to forget the wisdom of John Stuart Mill, when he said at St Andrews in 1867:

> Education makes a man a more intelligent shoemaker, if that be his occupation, but not by teaching him how to make shoes; it does so by the mental exercise it gives and the habits it impresses.

Index

Academic Board, 113–14
Admission of students, 39
A-level (GCE), 3, 96–8
    reform, 3, 96
Alexander, Lord, 5
Area boards, 61–5
A/S level (GCE), 3, 98

Boards, academic, 113–14
Boards, area, 61–5

Careers library, 51
Careers officers, 50–1
Centre for Policy Studies, 12
Certificate of Extended Education (CEE), 3, 8
Circulars (DES), 4, 36
City Technology Colleges, 122
Community links, 31–2
Consultation, public, 15, 17
Counselling, 50
Croydon, 2
Curriculum,
    breadth, 82
    description, 83
    objectives, 92
    organisation, 41

Departments, in FE, 35–7
    development, 35–6
    origins, 35
Departments, heads of, 37, 40–1, 42–3
Departments, in schools, 38
Department of Education and Science, 3, 5, 9, 11–12, 21–2,
    H.M. Inspectorate, in, 4, 10, 18, 21

Education Acts, 1, 9, 26
   1902 Act, 1
   1944 Act, 9, 26
   1980 Act, 9, 26
Education Bill (1988), 121
Examination reform, 3, 96–8
Examination results, 8
Exeter College, 5

Falling rolls, 14, 17, 33
Finsbury College, 35

General Certificate of Education (GCE),
   A level, 3, 96–8
   A/S level, 3, 96
Governing bodies, 26, 121

H. M. Inspectorate, 4, 10, 18, 21
   management review of, 10

Induction of students, 51–2
International Baccalaureate, 97

Liaison, 58–76
   between institutions, 61–5
   between teachers, 65–6
   with higher education, 70–2
   with the local community, 72–5
Liberal studies, 36
Luton Sixth Form College, 2

Macfarlane, N, 11
Macfarlane Report, 11
Magnus, P, 35
Manpower Services Commission, 33, 99, 110
Marketing, of colleges, 42
Mathematics, 35–6
Matrix structures, 29, 39
Meetings, 5, 18–19, 43, 45–6
   public, 18–19
   pupils, 5
   staff, 43, 45–6

NATFHE, 21
NCVQ, 94–5, 100, 122–3
NUT, 21

Oswestry, 102

Pastoral care, 20
Preston Sixth Form College, 6
Pupils meetings, 5

Qualifications,
   GCE (A level), 3, 96–8
   GCE (A/S level), 3, 96
   general, 95–6
   vocational, 94

Reorganisation of schools, 9–19, 23–5
   opposition to, 120–1
Review of colleges, 104–5
Richmond on Thames College, 6

Salaries, of teachers, 30–1
Schools Council, 3
Schools, departmental system, 38
Secondary school reorganisation, 9–11
   public consultation in, 15, 17
   public meetings in, 18–19
   timing of, 16, 23–5
Secretary of State (DES), 4, 9–10, 13, 18, 22
Sixth forms, 7–8, 63
Sixth form colleges, 2–4, 8, 87, 123
   courses, 3
   examination results, 8
   origins, 2
   size, 3
   social advantages of, 3
   student intake, 2
Special needs, 115–17
Staff, 29–31, 40, 43, 45–6, 108–9
   conditions of service, 29–30
   meetings, 43, 45–6
   roles, 29–30, 40
   salaries, 30–1
   support staff, 29, 108–9

Staffing structures, 11, 31
  of colleges, 31
  of schools, 11
Sunderland, 13–26

Teachers, 29–31, 40, 43, 45–6
  conditions of service, 29–30
  meetings, 43, 45–6
  roles, 29–30, 40
  salaries, 30–1
Tertiary colleges, 5–7, 27–8, 31, 33, 123
  definition of, 6–7
  development of, 6, 27–8
  history of, 5, 27, 33
  staffing of, 31
Tertiary reorganisation, 102, 120
  Manchester, 120
  Oswestry, 120
  Sheffield, 120
Tutors, 49–53, 55, 57
  training of, 57
Tutor groups, 53–3
Tutorial periods, 54–6
  for part-time students, 55–6
Tutorial systems, 48–9
TVEI, 32–3, 57, 121–2

Unions, 20–1, 114–15